Keith Didcock, Sam Pow,
Paul Sullivan & Nicola Williams

The publishers assert their right to use
Cool Camping as a trademark of Punk Publishing Ltd.

Cool Camping: France
First published in the United Kingdom in 2008 by
Punk Publishing Ltd
3 The Yard
Pegasus Place
London
SE11 5SD

www.punkpublishing.com

www.coolcamping.co.uk

A catalogue record of this book is available from the British Library.

ISBN-13: 978-0-9552036-5-7

10 9 8 7 6 5 4 3 2

Introduction 4
Getting There 8
Campsite Locator 10
Cool Camping Top 5 12
Campsites at a Glance 14
Brittany & Normandy 18
Around Paris 48
North Eastern France 54
The Alps 64
Central France 84
Burgundy 100
The Loire 114
The Atlantic Coast 126
Gers 146
The Dordogne & the Lot 152
The Pyrénées 172
Languedoc-Roussillon 192
Provence & Côte d'Azur 212
Useful Info 252
Useful Phrases 255

introduction

Bonjour et bienvenue à Cool Camping France!

If you thought camping in France was all about Europarks packed with Brits in socks and sandals, let *Cool Camping France* show you the path to a refreshingly different camping experience. From cosy six-tent snugs in Armagnac to a stylish, sustainable 600-pitch tentopolis in Brittany, this *is* camping enlightenment. And you can leave that '*Agadoo*' CD at home, thank you.

Camping in France can be a breeze. For the most part, the weather's better, the food's cheaper and the roads less congested than in the UK. The language is easy to grasp, too – many French words are simply English words said in a French accent – *le weekend, le web, le camping*. So that's the easy part. The hard part is finding those hidden, unique or spectacular places to stay, away from the corporate holiday parks that seem to dominate continental camping.

Thankfully, we've done the difficult bit for you. We've travelled thousands of miles, visited hundreds of campsites and eaten far more *baguettes* than should reasonably be consumed, all to bring you this very special selection of sites.

With this guide, you'll be able to pitch up in the grounds of a Louis XVI *château*, at the foot of Mont Blanc or amidst the volcanoes of the Massif Central. We've found shady riverside spots, remote unknown countryside hideaways – even a cliff-top site with an incredible vista of the French Riviera and sparkling blue Med. How about a tipi or a tree house? A Romany *roulotte,* a vintage Airstream trailer or an African desert tent? We've located them all for your camping pleasure.

Once you've chosen your spot, bashed in the tent pegs and paused for a sip of *vin rouge,* that's when the fun starts. *Cool Camping France* will have hardcore Alpinists heading for the heights, surfers riding Atlantic breakers and sky devils soaring with the birds in a paraglider or good old-fashioned hot-air balloon. Night-hiking in the Pyrénées, exploring 20,000-year-old cave paintings at Lascaux and panning for gold in Languedoc are hot pursuits for earthbound adventurers. And if this is all just too last year, novelty seekers can go and find out what ski-jöring is at the Ferme du Plantier near Lourdes.

But if your idea of a decent French holiday is nothing more than a Gallic shrug over a game of *boules* or kicking off your flip-flops, flopping in the sun and glugging a Côtes du Rhône between bites of *saucisson,* opportunities abound. Whether it's *camping à la ferme* (p252) between rolls of hay and grazing cows, out in the boonies with that back-to-nature feel or on your own deserted sliver of silver-sanded beach, there's a *Cool Camping* campsite for you.

And then there's the food. Forget food-miles, so local is the produce here, it's a case of food-metres. Not only are many *Cool Camping* sites in the heart of agricultural areas producing a dozen and one cheeses, *foie gras,* olive oil, champagne or Calvados – on many, owners grow their own, harvesting the fruits of the very trees shading your pitch. If things go bump in the night, it's usually an apple, almond or fat juicy cherry dropping on your tent! Every village has its own weekly food market spilling across a main square with a mouth-watering bounty of fruit and veg (some organic), as well as *charcuterie* (cold meats), *fromages* (cheeses), sometimes meat and fish, and always mountains of that irresistible French staple, *du pain* (bread). When you tire of DIY gourmandising, you'll find pointers to the odd Michelin-starred chef here too.

Our preference in this book has been for small, countryside, environmentally-conscious places or those with cracking views or something unique or special. Many of the best – like *Cool Camping's* Limousin tipis (p96) or our organic fruit-farm pick in the Pyrénées (p196) – are privately owned. But the weird and wonderful Huttopia chain of sites brings a refreshing new take on multi-site corporate ownership too. Wherever you choose to stay, rest assured that we'd happily return to every single one of these sites, so consider them a personal recommendation from us to you.

And so, *mes amis,* to the barricades! Brush off your phrasebook, wave *Au revoir* to pints of flat beer and driving on the left and off you go into the blue French yonder.

Bon voyage, campers, *bonne chance…*
et bon appetit!

getting there

Metaphorically speaking, France is now nearer than it's ever been before, with the short hop across *La Manche* (what the French call the English Channel) taking less time than a drive across London.

There are many ways of getting there – and if you're David Walliams you may even want to swim – but for us hopeless romantics at *Cool Camping*, braving the wild seas by boat, faithful Citroen packed with kit, is the way to go. Docking with great anticipation at port, sea salt on lips, you know you've arrived! And if that's not reason enough, we've even managed to negotiate a free bottle of plonk for *Cool Camping* readers who book with SeaFrance – see box opposite for more details.

The sleek Eurostar service from London's St-Pancras International is another option, but for campers with a car-load of kit, driving aboard a Eurotunnel train and whizzing through the Chunnel is a hassle-free, if fairly joyless experience.

It seems a bit of an environmental crime to fly such a short distance, and you'll probably need to rent a car at the other end anyway, but there are plenty of budget services serving most British airports.

However you go, return fares fluctuate hugely depending on how and when you book, what time of year and day you travel, how flexible a ticket you want, if you snag a special offer, and so on. A return ferry fare for car and passengers costs anything from £50 to £250, as does a return flight for one or a round trip on the Eurostar. Motoring through the Channel Tunnel can get the mob across for 100 quid return, but – as with ferries - there's still petrol 'n' *péages* (p252) to consider.

FERRIES

SeaFrance (0871 22 22 500; France 03 21 17 70 20; www.seafrance.com) Dover–Calais (1 h 15 min). The only French operator on this handy, short sea route. And don't forget to claim your free bottle of wine! (See right.)

P&O Ferries (08705 980 333; France 08 20 90 00 61; www.poferries.fr) Dover–Calais (1 h 30 min).

Norfolk Line (08708 701 020; France 00 44 8708 701 020; www.norfolkline-ferries.co.uk) Dover–Dunkirk (1 h 45 min).

Speed Ferries (0871 222 7456; France 00 44 8702 200 570; www.speedferries.com) Dover–Boulogne (50 minutes).

LD Lines (0844 576 88 36; France 08 25 304 304; www.ldlines.co.uk) Portsmouth–Le Havre (7 h 30 min) .

Transmanche Ferries (0800 9 171 201; France 08 00 65 01 00; www.transmancheferries.com) Newhaven–Dieppe (4 h), Newhaven–Le Havre (5 h, May–Sept only) and Portsmouth–Le Havre (7 h 30 min).

Brittany Ferries (0870 9 076 103; France 08 25 825 828; www.brittanyferries.com) Portsmouth–Caen (3 h 30 min or 7 h); Portsmouth–St-Malo (10 h 45 min); Portsmouth–Cherbourg (3 or 5 h); Poole–Cherbourg (2 h 30 min, 4 h 30 min or 6 h 30 min), Plymouth–Roscoff (6 or 8 h).

Condor Ferries (0870 2 435 140; France 08 25 16 54 63; www.condorferries.fr) Weymouth–St-Malo (5 h 15 min).

TRAINS

Eurotunnel (08705 35 35 35; France 08 10 63 03 04; www.eurotunnel.com) Drive aboard a shuttle in Folkestone and emerge 35 minutes later in Calais.

Eurostar (08705 186 186, France 00 44 1233 617 575, www.eurostar.com) High-speed rail travel from St-Pancras International and Ashford to Calais (1 h), Lille (1 h 25 min), Paris Gare de Nord (2 h 15 min) and Avignon (6 h 15 min).

SNCF (www.voyages-sncf.com) French national railways.

PLANES

British Airways (www.britishairways.com) and **Air France** (www.airfrance.fr) zip between the UK and France. Paris airports Orly and Charles de Gaulle (www.aeroportsdeparis.fr) are well connected by rail with central Paris, but Beauvais (www.aeroportbeauvais.com), 65 miles north, is a 1 h 15-minute trek by coach.

Easyjet (0905 821 0905; France 08 99 65 00 11; www.easyjet.com) No-frill flights from London Gatwick, Luton, Stansted and other regional UK airports to Paris Charles de Gaulle and Orly, Lyon, Grenoble, La Rochelle, Bordeaux, Toulouse and Nice.

Ryanair (0871 246 000; France 08 92 23 23 75; www.ryanair.com) Budget airline flying from Stansted, Luton, East Midlands, Liverpool, Bristol and Glasgow to Paris Beauvais and many French regional airports, including Poitiers, La Rochelle, Rodez, Perpignan, Carcassonne, Bergerac, Pau and Grenoble.

DON'T FORGET YOUR VA VA VOOM

If you're taking your car, fit headlamp converters before crossing the Channel; slap on a GB sticker if your number plate doesn't feature the EU circle of stars; check weather conditions on the French roads (00 33 892 68 08 08); and find out where you're going (www.viamichelin.co.uk). Oh yes, and drive on the right when you get there. That bit's important.

campsite locator

MAP	CAMPSITE	LOCATION	PAGE
1	Étretat	Brittany & Normandy	18
2	Le Brévedent	Brittany & Normandy	22
3	La Pointe	Brittany & Normandy	26
4	Camping du Letty	Brittany & Normandy	30
5	Bois des Écureuils	Brittany & Normandy	34
6	Château du Deffay	Brittany & Normandy	36
7	Les Tipis du Bonheur de Vivre	Brittany & Normandy	40
8	Kota Cabana	Brittany & Normandy	42
9	Forest View	Brittany & Normandy	46
10	Huttopia Versailles	Around Paris	48
11	Camping de Troyes	North Eastern France	54
12	Les Grèbes du Lac de Marcenay	North Eastern France	56
13	Domaine du Haut des Bluches	North Eastern France	62
14	Le Grand Champ	The Alps	64
15	Le Prieuré	The Alps	70
16	Ferme Noemie	The Alps	74
17	La Source	The Alps	80
18	Les Roulottes de la Serve	Central France	84
19	Indigo Royat	Central France	88
20	Près des Étangs	Central France	92
21	Les Chenauds	Central France	94
22	Tipis At Folbeix	Central France	96
23	Camping des 2 Rives	Burgundy	100
24	La Forêt du Morvan	Burgundy	104
25	Camping de Nevers	Burgundy	110
26	Hortus, Le Jardin de Sully	The Loire	114
27	Les Roulottes	The Loire	116
28	Le Moulin Fort	The Loire	122
29	La Vendette	The Atlantic Coast	126
30	Les Sables d'Argent	The Atlantic Coast	132
31	Panorama du Pyla	The Atlantic Coast	136
32	Cap de l'Homy	The Atlantic Coast	142
33	Domaine Le Poteau	Gers	146
34	La Brouquère	Gers	148
35	Les Ormes	The Dordogne & the Lot	152
36	Le Petit Lion	The Dordogne & the Lot	156
37	Camping de L'îlot	The Dordogne & the Lot	160
38	Le Capeyrou	The Dordogne & the Lot	164
39	Camping de l'Ouysse	The Dordogne & the Lot	168
40	Camping Pyrénées Natura	The Pyrénées	172
41	Ferme du Plantier	The Pyrénées	176
42	Tipis Indiens	The Pyrénées	180
43	Les Tilleuls	The Pyrénées	184
44	BelRepayre Trailer Park	The Pyrénées	186
45	Val d'Aleth	Languedoc-Roussillon	192
46	Mas de la Fargassa	Languedoc-Roussillon	196
47	Les Criques de Porteils	Languedoc-Roussillon	200
48	Indigo Rieumontagné	Languedoc-Roussillon	204
49	Les Chalets du Tarn	Languedoc-Roussillon	206
50	La Corconne	Languedoc-Roussillon	208
51	Beau Rivage	Provence & Côte d'Azur	212
52	Le Clapas	Provence & Côte d'Azur	214
53	Les Roulottes de Saint-Cerice	Provence & Côte d'Azur	220
54	Les Oliviers	Provence & Côte d'Azur	222
55	Les Matherons	Provence & Côte d'Azur	226
56	Camping des Gorges du Verdon	Provence & Côte d'Azur	230
57	Domaine Chasteuil-Provence	Provence & Côte d'Azur	234
58	Les Gorges du Loup	Provence & Côte d'Azur	240
59	La Camassade	Provence & Côte d'Azur	242
60	Les Romarins	Provence & Côte d'Azur	246

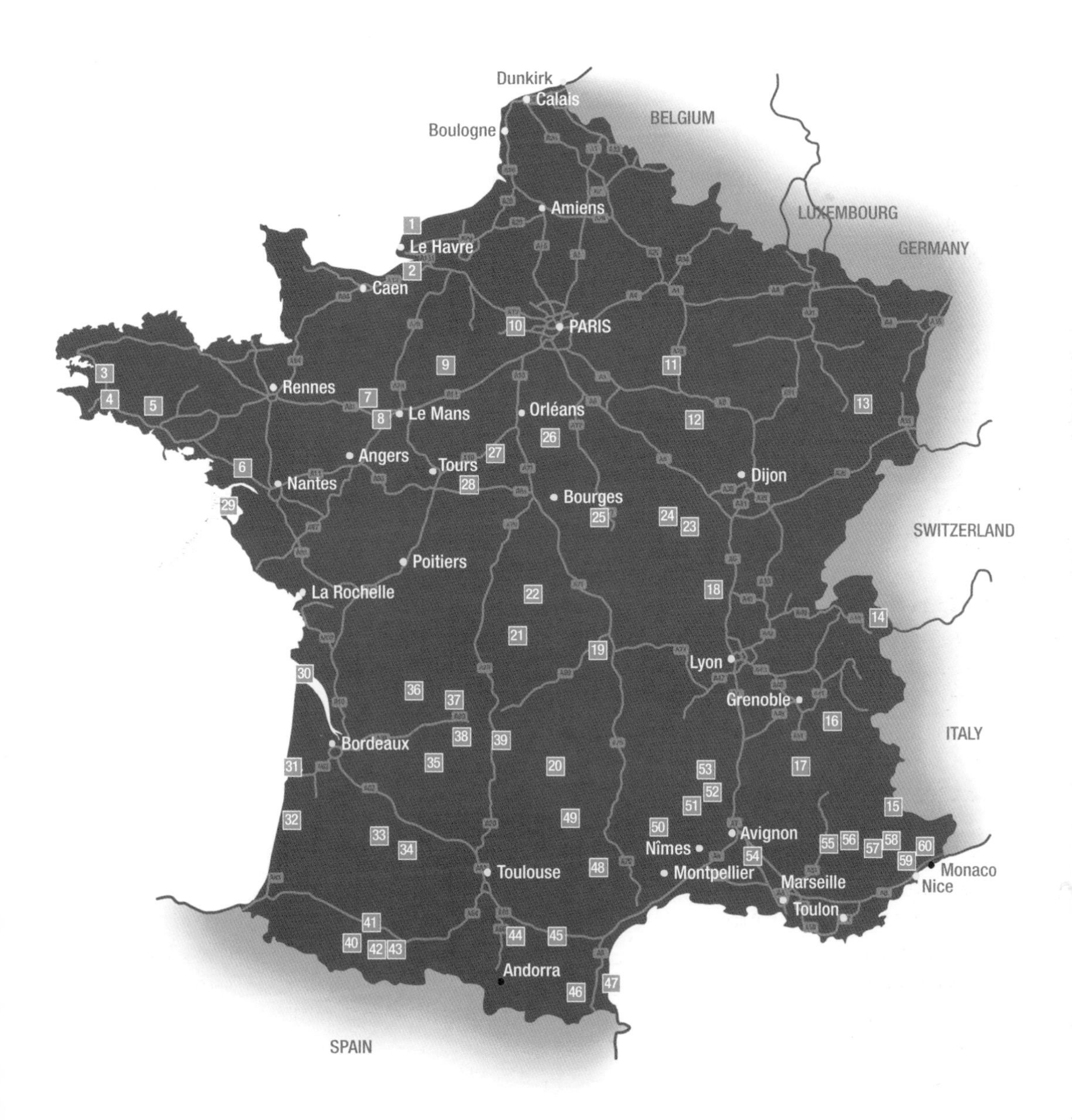

Dunkirk
Calais
Boulogne
BELGIUM
LUXEMBOURG
GERMANY
Amiens
Le Havre
Caen
PARIS
Rennes
Le Mans
Orléans
Angers
Tours
Nantes
Dijon
Bourges
SWITZERLAND
Poitiers
La Rochelle
Lyon
Grenoble
Bordeaux
ITALY
Avignon
Nîmes
Montpellier
Toulouse
Marseille
Toulon
Monaco
Nice
Andorra
SPAIN
1
2
3
4
5
6
7
8
9
10
11
12
13
14
15
16
17
18
19
20
21
22
23
24
25
26
27
28
29
30
31
32
33
34
35
36
37
38
39
40
41
42
43
44
45
46
47
48
49
50
51
52
53
54
55
56
57
58
59
60

Quechua
1
2
3
4

cool camping top 5

It's always tough picking the best of the best. But there has to be an ultimate winner of winners, an overlord to aspire to, a Jedi master of French campsites. To paraphrase the Sith Lord, *the force is strong with these ones.*

1 Les Romarins p246

Perfectly positioned between high-rolling Monte Carlo and sophisticated Nice, this Riviera beauty has million-dollar Med views.

2 Le Brévedent p22

Château camping in the grounds of a Louis XVIth hunting lodge with pitches by the lake or amongst the apple trees.

3 BelRepayre Trailer Park p186

Stay onboard a slick 70s caravan, get down to DJ Bobby Lotion's disco 45s, and live the retro dream. Groooovy baby.

4 Les Tilleuls p184

Valley views. Mammoth mountains. Chilled camping. *C'est tout!*

5= Le Grand Champ p64

Big old mountains all around and Mont Blanc just a short trek away. Could this be the pinnacle of Alpine campsites?

5= Tipis at Folbeix p96

Environmentally friendly living in stylish, secluded tipis scattered around an enchanted forest.

VAUDE

campsites at a glance

COOL FOR CAMPFIRES

- 10 Huttopia Versailles 48
- 23 Camping des 2 Rives 100
- 27 Les Roulottes 116
- 42 Tipis Indiens 180

STUNNING VIEWS

- 1 Étretat 18
- 29 La Vendette 126
- 31 Panorama du Pyla 136
- 40 Camping Pyrénées Natura 172
- 42 Tipis Indiens 180
- 60 Les Romarins 246

FOR FIRST-TIME CAMPERS

- 2 Le Brévedent 22
- 4 Camping du Letty 30
- 10 Huttopia Versailles 48
- 13 Domaine des Haut du Bluches 62
- 28 Le Moulin Fort 122
- 51 Beau Rivage 212
- 57 Domaine Chasteuil-Provence 234

MIDDLE OF NOWHERE

- 20 Près des Étangs 92
- 21 Les Chenauds 94
- 22 Tipis at Folbeix 96
- 46 Mas de la Fargassa 196
- 55 Les Matherons 226

CHÂTEAU-TASTIC!

- 6 Château de Deffay 36
- 26 Hortus, Le Jardin de Sully 114
- 27 Les Roulottes 116
- 34 La Brouquère 148
- 38 Le Capeyrou 164
- 44 BelRepayre Trailer Park 186

BEACH WITHIN REACH

- 1 Étretat 18
- 3 La Pointe 26
- 4 Camping du Letty 30
- 29 La Vendette 126
- 31 Panorama du Pyla 136
- 32 Cap de l'Homy 142
- 37 Camping de L'îlot 160
- 47 Les Criques de Porteils 200
- 52 Le Clapas 214

SURF'S UP

- 32 Cap de l'Homy 142
- 60 Les Romarins 246

LAKESIDE CHILLING

- 6 Château du Deffay 36
- 12 Les Grèbes du lac de Marcenay 56
- 20 Près des Étangs 92
- 21 Les Chenauds 94
- 35 Les Ormes 152
- 37 Camping de L'îlot 160
- 48 Indigo Rieumontagné 204
- 51 Beau Rivage 212

FINE FOR WINE

- 12 Les Grèbes du Lac de Marcenay 56
- 18 Les Roulóttes de la Serve 84
- 23 Camping des 2 Rives 100
- 26 Hortus, Le Jardin de Sully 114
- 28 Le Moulin Fort 122
- 30 Les Sables d'Argent 132
- 33 Domaine Le Poteau 146
- 34 La Brouquère 148
- 35 Les Ormes 152
- 36 Le Petit Lion 156
- 45 Val d'Aleth 192

CAMPING À LA FERME

- 16 Ferme Noemie 74
- 34 La Brouquère 148
- 39 Camping de l'Ouysse 168
- 41 Ferme du Plantier 176
- 46 Mas de la Fargassa 196

HIGH ON MOUNTAINS

- 14 Le Grand Champ 64
- 15 Le Prieuré 70
- 16 Ferme Noemie 74
- 19 Indigo Royat 88
- 40 Camping Pyrénées Natura 172
- 42 Tipis Indiens 180
- 43 Les Tilleuls 184

FOR CAR-LESS CAMPERS

10 Huttopia Versailles 48
11 Camping de Troyes 54
26 Hortus, Le Jardin de Sully 114
38 Le Capeyrou 164
54 Les Oliviers 222

A FRIENDLY WELCOME

2 Le Brévedent 22
3 La Pointe 26
4 Camping du Letty 30
11 Camping de Troyes 54
12 Les Grèbes du lac de Marcenay 56
16 Ferme Noemie 74
22 Tipis at Folbeix 96
45 Val d'Aleth 192

GOOD FOR KIDS

3 La Pointe 26
4 Camping du Letty 30
10 Huttopia Versailles 48
11 Camping de Troyes 54
19 Indigo Royat 88
28 Le Moulin Fort 122
31 Panorama du Pyla 136
35 Les Ormes 152
36 Le Petit Lion 156
47 Les Criques de Porteils 200
48 Indigo Rieumontagné 204
58 Les Gorges du Loup 240

WET 'N' WILD

4 Camping du Letty 30
20 Près des Étangs 92
30 Les Sables d'Argent 132
35 Les Ormes 152
48 Indigo Rieumontagné 204

ROMANTIC RETREAT

8 Kota Cabana 42
18 Les Roulottes de la Serve 84
22 Tipis at Folbeix 96
39 Camping de l'Oussye 168
34 La Brouquère 148
44 BelRepayre Trailer Park 186
60 Les Romarins 246

WALK THIS WAY

15 La Prieuré 70
24 La Forêt du Morvan 104
28 Le Moulin Fort 122
36 Le Petit Lion 156
40 Camping Pyrénées Natura 172
41 Ferme du Plantier 176
46 Mas de la Fargassa 196

RIVERSIDE CHILLING

28 Le Moulin Fort 122
37 Camping de L'îlot 160
39 Camping de l'Ouysse 168
49 Les Chalets du Tarn 206
50 La Corconne 208
51 Beau Rivage 212

FOREST FUN

5 Bois des Écureuils 34
9 Forest View 46
22 Tipis at Folbeix 96
24 La Forêt du Morvan 104
28 Le Moulin Fort 122
49 Les Chalets du Tarn 206
50 La Corconne 208

FISH CLUB

11 Camping de Troyes 54
31 Panorama du Pyla 136
48 Indigo Rieumontagné 204

ON YER BIKE

16 Ferme Noemie 74
23 Camping des 2 Rives 100
28 Le Moulin Fort 122
30 Les Sables d'Argent 132
41 Ferme du Plantier 176

SOMETHING DIFFERENT

7 Les Tipis du Bonheur de Vivre 40
8 Kota Cabana 42
18 Les Roulottes de la Serve 84
22 Tipis at Folbeix 96
27 Les Roulottes 116
33 Domaine Le Poteau 146
42 Tipis Indiens 180
44 BelRepayre Trailer Park 186

MAIRIE
Moules

étretat

The 19th-century writer Guy de Maupassant spent his early years living in the Villa des Verguies in Étretat. There he befriended the English poet Charles Algernon Swinburne, who, it was claimed, lived with an ape called Nip and was in the habit of eating roast monkey for supper. Whatever the truth of such calumnies, Nip avoided the pot, only to be hanged by a vindictive servant. Swinburne had him buried under a granite headstone that doubled as a birdbath, leaving a rueful Maupassant to comment that geniuses never have healthy minds.

Étretat may no longer be the haunt of poetic *flâneurs* with pantries full of edible simian but it does retain some of the mystical allure that attracted Swinburne in the first place. It's also a handy place to stop for your first night on French soil, being only 15 miles (24 km) up the Normandy coast from the ferry terminal at Le Havre. And, in contrast to the concrete modernism of that city (don't snigger – it's a UNESCO World Heritage Site), Étretat is a pleasing mixture of an old medieval centre, complete with a covered wooden market with a selection of distinguished *belle époque* residential villas. It was this more civilised aspect of the town that attracted Monet, who came to paint the town's shingle beach and magnificent chalky cliffs.

And you'll soon see why. If you climb the steps at the north of the town up onto the sea cliff, you'll find that whole place fits almost perfectly onto a modest-sized canvas. You can see the town pressing up against the broad promenade and the curve of the shore, dotted with boats pulled up above the tideline, and the naturally eroded arch in the white cliff edging out to sea. Up on top of the cliff is a golf course not best suited to those with vertigo or a wicked slice. In fact, the white gleam in the sea when the sun shines might just as well be the reflection of a seabed of lost golf balls as the remains of the crumbling white cliffs.

The Normandy coast is well-known for its towns, ports and, of course, the D-Day beaches. It's where James Bond encounters Le Chiffre in the fictional town of Royale-les-Eaux (based on the real-life Deauville) at the start of *Casino Royale*. Étretat may not be a port and it doesn't have a casino but a few miles up the coast is the neat little town of Fécamp, which has both. The small harbour dates back to the Dark Ages and was once a favourite anchorage of the

Vikings. Apparently even centuries ago, the fishing fleet used to range as far as Newfoundland for months at a stretch in search of the tastiest *fruits de mer*. Luckily you won't have to travel so far nowadays, as there's a little restaurant in town called L'Escalier, which serves delicious *moules* steamed in cider or calvados. It's a reminder too that Normandy is apple country and whilst eaten raw they may keep the doctor away, they're much more enticing when fortified or fermented.

Back in Étretat, you'll find the municipal campsite a short walk from the seafront along rue Guy de Maupassant. Given that reminder of the town's louche past, it's a relief to find that the site is an oasis of sanity and order. It's a compact and beautifully maintained little place with a dedicated tent camping area between the shrubs towards the rear, at the foot of a wooded hill. And don't worry – there aren't any monkeys lurking in the trees.

THE UPSIDE: A 10-minute walk to one of the finest seaside towns on the Normandy coast.

THE DOWNSIDE: It has a municipal liking for the rules.

THE DAMAGE: Car and tent €3.10, caravan €3.60 plus €3.10 per adult and €1.90 per child (4–10 years). Electricity €4.50–5.40, depending on ampage.

THE FACILITIES: Male and female toilets, hot showers and washing facilities. The fact that the facilities are behind a combination-lock gate should tell you that they are clean and well looked after.

FOOD AND DRINK: Le Clos Lupin (37 rue Alphonse Karr; 00 33 2 35 29 67 53) does a great *tournedos de canard*. For drinks, try La Rose des Vents, a shop on the corner of rue Monge and rue de l'Abbé Cochet, for a wide array of Normandy ciders.

FAMILY FUN: There's a *vélorail* (that's right, a pedal-powered railway) running 5 miles (8 km) from Étretat to Les Loges. Because, let's face it, someone could probably use the exercise.

TREAT YOURSELF: If you've a head for heights, try the cliff-top golf course (00 33 2 35 27 04 89) – one of the top 25 courses in France – followed by a 19th-hole stop at Dormy House (00 33 2 35 27 07 88), a magnificent hotel with panoramic views over the beach.

GETTING THERE: From Le Havre take the D940 up the coast, following the signs for Étretat. Enter the town down a long hill and turn right at the traffic lights opposite the Marie. Follow rue Guy de Maupassant about half a mile (nearly 1 km) and the campsite is on the left.

OPEN: Mid-Mar–mid-Oct.

IF IT'S FULL: A further 10 miles (16 km) up the coast is Fécamp, which has a dramatic campsite set into the slopes above the beach. Domaine de Reneville (chemin de Nesmond; 00 33 2 35 28 20 97; campingdereneville.free.fr).

Camping Municipal d'Étretat, rue Guy de Maupassant, 76790 Étretat | t | 00 33 2 35 27 07 67

le brévedent

This is surely one of the classiest campsites in France. Set in the grounds of a Louis XVIth hunting lodge, with pitches around a mirrored lake, amidst apple trees and on the fringe of a wood, the *château* of Le Brévedent has been in the same family for 400 years and has been used for camping for four generations. Raphaël Guerrey, who has recently taken over the running of the place from his mother, runs the site with his wife and small (fifth-generation) son.

Camping came about at Le Brévedent in part because of the ruination caused by the Second World War. The lodge had been occupied by the Germans and was badly damaged when a passing Allied bomber inadvertently dropped its payload on its way to crashing in the woods. In order to help pay for the repairs, the Marquis de Chabannes La Palice – Raphaël's great-grandfather – decided to plant apple trees to harvest the fruit, began extracting lime from the woods to sell to local farmers and invited campers to come and stay in the grounds.

Further encouragement came in the form of an organisation set up in 1957 by Georges Pilliet to help the owners of French *châteaux* preserve their family heritage. Le Brévedent became a member of the Castel group of campsites in 1965 and now looks upon the fellow owners as a second family. If only something similar had happened back home we could all be camping on the lawns at Chatsworth and Cliveden right now.

Of course, there was a little added cachet at Le Brévedent, as the idea of staying with a French Marquis proved an unsurprising hit. It did lead some campers into delusions of grandeur, however. One early visitor was discomfited to discover that dinner jackets were not obligatory evening attire. He had assumed that dinner with the Marquis required a certain degree of formality.

Rest assured there's no dress code here now, and you'll find a welcoming, laid-back attitude from everyone you meet. The Guerrey family are endlessly entertaining companions for an evening in the bar in the lodge, which Raphaël opens every night from 9pm. Whether it's the history of the lodge, the family – which traces its roots back 1000 years – French politics or the deficiencies of British farming, they're happy to chat to their guests, many of whom are now such regular visitors as to consider Le Brévedent a second home. Raphaël's also a talented musician and is partial to jamming with anyone who happens along with a guitar. In fact, he's even gone so far as to organise musical evenings in front of the floodlit house for anyone who wishes to participate.

The sessions don't last too long into the night, though, and you're more likely to be disturbed by the plop of the occasional apple dropping from the trees onto the grass than by anything else. And when morning comes, you'll probably be roused by the sound of the baker's van arriving with the first batch of fresh bread. If the sound doesn't get you, the smell will. Try staying in your sleeping bag when the aroma of warm *pains au chocolat*, still soft and gooey from the oven, is wafting across the grass. You'll be up like a shot and climbing into your *culottes* before you can say '*sacre bleu!*'.

Still, it'll be the only time in your stay at Le Brévedent when you break into more than an amble. That's just the kind of place it is. Because when you've been around for as long as this place has, what's the hurry?

THE UPSIDE: A fascinating family, a beautiful house, a lake and a garden full of apple trees.

THE DOWNSIDE: It's hard to think of one.

THE DAMAGE: €9 for a tent or caravan (€7 in May, June and September) plus €6.70 per adult (€5.20 low season); €6.70 per child (7–12 years) (€3.35); and €3.50 per younger child (€2.20). Electricity is €3.20 or €2.45 per night, depending on the season.

THE FACILITIES: Immaculate. One of the newly decorated blocks could grace the pages of an interior design magazine. Good hot showers, pearly white lavatories and plenty of washing facilities.

FOOD AND DRINK: The usual *boulangerie*, *pâtisserie*, and so on can be found in the charming village of Blangy-le-Château. The small bar in the lodge sells cider made by a local farmer called Edward Maclean (yes, he's originally from Scotland). While you're here, try the brew called Apéro, a mixture of cider, blackcurrant and calvados; it might sound like snakebite but it's far classier. There is also a restaurant on site but if you want something special, see TREAT YOURSELF below.

FAMILY FUN: There are two children's play areas on the site with swings, climbing frames and a roundabout. In the gardens there's an ancient tree that's great for climbing; if that's not enough, the Kids' Club organises daily activities.

TREAT YOURSELF: To a slap-up meal. A former one-star Michelin chef called Bernard Vaxelaire, having tired of the glitz and glamour of his Paris restaurant, runs a fantastic place called Les Gourmandises (rue de l'Abbaye; 00 33 2 32 42 10 96) in the nearby town of Cormeilles.

GETTING THERE: Take the A13 *autoroute* from Paris (or join it from the A29 over the Pont de Normandie from Le Havre), heading for Pont l'Évêque. Take the D579 for just over a mile (2 km) and turn left for Manneville-la-Pipard. Follow the road to Blangy-le-Château and turn right in the village and Le Brévedent is just over a mile (2 km) down the road. The site is on the left, just after the road leading to the church.

OPEN: Late-Apr–Sept.

IF IT'S FULL: There's another Castel Camping site at Château Le Colombier (14590 Moyaux; 00 33 2 31 63 63 08), about 6 miles (10 km) to the southwest. It's slightly larger but the same idea, set between a *château* and an ornate dovecote.

Castel Camping Le Brévedent, 14130 Le Brévedent | t | 00 33 2 31 64 72 88 | w | www.campinglebrevedent.com

La Pointe
Superbe Camping
Rte St. Coulitz

la pointe

Like the latest 3G, wi-fi, 4 mega-pixel, mp3-playing mobile phone with optional cardiac defibrillator, western Brittany may appear to some as over-engineered. It seems to have bagged more than its fair share of what technophiles call functionality. It has rolling hills of heather and pine, extravagant cliff-fringed sandy bays, ancient hilltop towns, lazy tree-lined rivers and towns bedecked with floral window boxes. But, then, who's complaining? And, if you come to La Pointe, you'll get the bonus feature of having all this and more within a short drive.

La Pointe sits just outside the quiet and picturesque town of Châteaulin, around a long bend in a canalised section of the River Aulne, which empties into the Brest basin. The site's stamp of authenticity is that, although it is owned by a British couple, it attracts a loyal following of French regulars – families in the busy months of July and August and the *troisième âge* crew out of season. And it's easy to see why. At the foot of a forest and with a sprinkling stream (perfect for cooling your beer and keeping your butter hard) running down its flank, the site is as spacious as the countryside around it.

The pitches are on the generous side of huge, with each of them separated by a little hedge for privacy. But if you want to get away from it all, there are grassy terraces cut into the wooded hillside above the camp where you can really spread out. It's just a shame that you can't linger too long, lounging around in the trees, because there's just too much to do.

To get a real impression of the Breton countryside, take the trip up to the summit of Ménez Hom. You can drive most of it and just walk up the slope to the trigonometric point at the top. From here there's a 360° panorama of western Brittany – from the outline of Brest to the north, down the dramatic coastline to Douarnenez, over the rolling hills to the south towards Quimper and back up the valley carved out of the land by the Aulne. You're likely to find your eyes drawn to the alluring shores of the Baie de Douarnenez and, before you know it, you'll probably be rolling back down the hill towards the beaches.

These extravagantly long stretches of sand, particularly the huge bay at Pentrez, are ideal for wind-powered beach craft. You'll occasionally see one whizzing silently about and you'll need to keep well out of the way – they can reach eye-watering speeds. If you prefer to avoid the beach-borne traffic, then head to Trez Bellec a little farther north. It's a smaller and more intimate beach than Pentrez, more a bucket-and-spade than a boy-racer kind of place and just the spot to while away an afternoon.

And when you're feeling a little peckish, you'll want to get to the town of Locronan for tea. Park the car outside the town because the centre is traffic-free. This place dates back 2500 years and is so reminiscent of the Cotswolds that it's a favourite location for filmmakers (it was used, for example, in Roman Polanski's version of Hardy's novel *Tess of the d'Urbevilles*). Christianised by Saint Ronan in the 9th century, there's a long Celtic tradition here and then, because of the abundance of hemp grown in the vicinity, in the 14th century the town became famous for making sailcloth. Now, it's a cobbled and car-free haven and just perfect to enjoy a cup of tea opposite the 15th-century granite church.

And, finally, it's back to La Pointe, where the sun's about to go down, the mist is starting to drift across the river and darkness is creeping about in the trees. There's just time to fish that nicely chilled beer from the stream and sit under the brightening stars for a while before turning in for a night of well-deserved rest. Tomorrow, as they say, is another day.

THE UPSIDE: Superbly appointed site with quiet forest pitches and well-kept gardens.

THE DOWNSIDE: There's a (very quiet) road between the campsite and the river.

THE DAMAGE: A tent and 2 adults is €12.50. A caravan/camper plus 2 is €15. Additional adults are €4 and children under 10 are €2. Electricity is €2.50.

THE FACILITIES: Good clean facilities block with plenty of hot showers and toilets. Separate areas for washing dishes and clothes. There's also an information room with details of local attractions.

FOOD & DRINK: There is a sizeable Intermarché supermarket up the hill out of town. For dining, head for Le Miniscule on rue Baltzer in Châteaulin (00 33 2 98 86 28 66). There's a terrace out front if the weather's good but there's a much nicer little restaurant area with leather banquettes and wicker chairs through the back. Their Franco-Mex *fruits de mer* tortilla *entrée* is the pick of an eclectic menu.

FAMILY FUN: Take the kids to Aquarive at Quimper (Route de Kerogan, Creac'h Gwen, 29000 Quimper; 00 33 2 98 52 00 15). This huge indoor aqua sports centre has giant slides, hot pools, saunas and a solarium.

TREAT YOURSELF: To a spot of paragliding. If you've a head for heights and a sense of adventure, you can paraglide from the summit of Ménez Hom. From April to September, Club Celtic de Vol Libre (00 33 2 98 81 50 27; www.vol-libre-menez-hom.com) runs courses from three to 20 hours for beginners to experts. It costs anything from €50 to €300.

GETTING THERE: From Rennes, follow the N12 for about 15 miles (24 km) and then take the N164, signposted for Quimper. Stay on this road all the way to Châteaulin (it's over 100 miles/ 160 km). Follow the road down the hill to the river in the centre of town. Turn left and then right over the bridge. Turn left on the other side and follow the river to where the road forks. Take the left fork, following the road along the river for about half a mile (nearly 1 km). The campsite is signposted to the left. Follow the road for 45 metres and La Pointe is on your right.

OPEN: Mid-Apr–Oct.

IF IT'S FULL: Your best bet is to head to one of the sites next to the beach at Trez Bellec Plage, the nicest of which is Camping Le Panoramic (29560 Telgruc-sur-Mer; 00 33 2 98 27 78 41; www.camping-panoramic.com).

La Pointe, Route St Coulitz, 29150 Châteaulin	t	00 33 2 98 86 51 53	w	www.lapointesuperbecamping.com

camping du letty

Bénodet is a little reminiscent of Amityville, the summer holiday town from the *Jaws* films – though without the great white shark. It has the same flurry of activity when the sun shines, but you know it's reliant on the tourists (and a little bit of fishing) to see it through the winter months. But come here in the summer and you'll enjoy a bustling little town set along a curving bay, with an attractive marina in the mouth of the River Odet and a lighthouse that winks flirtatiously at every passing vessel after dark.

A short way along the *corniche* from the shops and restaurants is Camping du Letty, run by two generations of the Le Guyader family. Marc and his parents have their work cut out here as the site is enormous – over 25 acres with about 600 pitches. But don't be put off by the size of the place, as the abundant hedges give each area such a sense of privacy and seclusion that you could easily forget that you're in the midst of a huge tentopolis.

It's so large, in fact, that there are six washing blocks around the site, one of which has been cunningly built out of a German gun emplacement from the Second World War. It gives Monsieur Le Guyader senior a certain wicked pleasure to tell guests that it's been turned into a *pissoir*.

The site abuts Plage du Groasguan, which may sound like an unappealingly thin porridge, but is actually a strip of golden sand next to a slinky little lagoon. Across the placid water is a long finger of sand, known as the Dunes Domaniales de Mousterlin, which blocks out the worst of the sea's swell. The result is a perfect backwater, ideal for launching the kids out onto the not-so-high seas with one of the local sailing schools to learn the difference between running on a beam reach and turning turtle. Landlubber parents in the meantime can relax on the beach and soak up the sun without having to worry about their little ones being blown by the trade winds half way to the Azores.

And after a hard day on the beach, head back into town and you'll be intrigued by some of the local architecture. The most obvious landmark, apart from the flirty lighthouse, is the *folie de grandeur* of a large white house built in the shape of a ship. Now, there always seems to be something a little strange about buildings in the shape of ships. They conjure up images of some long-retired Rear Admiral donning a moth-eaten uniform each morning and stepping out onto the balcony to run a flag up the mast and take a bearing. Humpf, he'll say. Same as yesterday. And the day before. Odd.

As you stroll along, you'll also notice the attractive art deco beachside changing rooms below the promenade, with sheet-steel doors and small windows of brightly coloured glass bricks. And if you carry on past Pointe du Coq, you'll be on your way to the old port of Bénodet, where the river cruisers will take you upstream to Quimper. It's another stretch of quiet water that serves as a marina for the flotilla of pleasure boats that abound in the area. The old port is the place to come if you want to buy some fresh seafood, just off the boat and possibly still staring at you in surprise, to take back to the Letty to fry up in some butter and white wine.

THE UPSIDE: Shady and private pitches slap bang on a sheltered sandy inlet.

THE DOWNSIDE: Its size – not what you could call intimate.

THE DAMAGE: A pitch for a tent, caravan or camper is €9 whatever the season with an additional charge of €2 for a car or camper. Prices per adult range from €4 to €6.50 depending on the season and from €2 to €3.25 for up to six-year-olds. The price of electricity depends on ampage and season and ranges from €1.50 for a 1-amp flicker in June to €4 for a 4-amp buzz in August.

THE FACILITIES: There are six *blocs sanitaires* around the site with everything you need (including separate showers to wash your dog, if you so wish) and all of a reasonable standard but a hot shower will cost you €0.60. In addition, there are saunas, a solarium, a jacuzzi, a gym...in fact, you name it.

FOOD AND DRINK: There are bars and restaurants along the seafront but for something altogether better, head to the old port where the restaurant at the Hôtel l'Abbatiale (00 33 2 98 66 21 66) specialises in the day's catch. If you're there early enough in the evening, there's a small fish shop around the side of the hotel if you fancy frying your own and a Champion supermarket on the edge of town.

FAMILY FUN: Try the sailing schools on the water behind the large sand dune. It's a nice sheltered place for kids to venture out on the not-so-high seas. Details can be obtained from the campsite.

TREAT YOURSELF: To a boat trip up the Odet to Quimper. There are several companies offering the trip but the best one is probably the *croisière gastronomique* run by Vendettes de l'Odet (00 33 2 98 57 00 58), which serves a sumptuous seafood lunch on board for €24.

GETTING THERE: From Quimper to the north, take the D34 and follow the signs for Bénodet. At the roundabout called Rond Point Ty Pin, bear left onto Route du Letty, carry onto rue du Canvez and take the second left down chemin de Creisanguer. The site entrance is at the end of the road.

OPEN: Mid-June to September.

IF IT'S FULL: According to Mme Le Guyader, it's only full about once every 10 years. However, Camping Pointe St Gilles is just next door in an emergency.

Camping du Letty, 29950 Bénodet | t 00 33 2 98 57 04 69 | w www.campingduletty.com

BOIS DES
ECUREUILS

bois des écureuils

Squirrels, seals and puppy dogs all seem to have a way of tugging at human heart-strings, which, in the case of squirrels at least, is rather odd as they're part of the rodent family. Nevertheless, there's a reason to seek out the campsite of Bois des Écureuils (that's Squirrel Wood in English) and that's because France has been spared the ravages of the grey squirrel and still has its smaller and much cuter red cousin.

This small, discreet site is tucked neatly, squirreled away even, into the farmlands of southern Brittany. With only 40 pitches, this British-owned site is quite snug and fairly rural but offers great opportunities for some solitude, if that's what you're after. As the name implies, the site's main attraction is its woodland (a glorious mixture of oak, beech, birch and chestnut) and, if you're lucky and keep really still, its squirrels.

Nearby, the curiously named village of Guilligomarc'h, with its honey-coloured stone and white-painted shutters, is a quaint, quiet and typically Breton place with friendly locals. If after a couple of days of peace and quiet you're itching for something to do, the nearby Scorff and Ellé rivers provide some spectacular scenery (check out the road along the river through the Forêt de Pont-Calleck) along with a few scary places, such as the Devil's Rocks north of Locunolé, which is a favourite spot for canoeing enthusiasts who like their water as white as it comes and very much on the rocks.

THE UPSIDE: Seclusion and tranquillity in a woodland setting.

THE DOWNSIDE: Other than the scenery, there are few other attractions nearby.

THE DAMAGE: €5 for a pitch and €3 per adult and €1.50 per child. Electric hook-ups are an additional €2.50.

THE FACILITIES: A decent, clean block with plenty of toilets and hot showers. Plus, a handy washing machine.

FOOD AND DRINK: There is a small shop on site for the basics. Both the nearby villages of Guilligomarc'h and Arzano have *boulangeries* and *pâtisseries*, but if you're staying a few days then stock up before you arrive as there's not much nearby in terms of bars and restaurants.

FAMILY FUN: There are bikes for hire at the site. This is quiet farming country so the roads aren't busy and lend themselves to the more leisurely kind of cycling, a far cry from the Tour de France, which passes by some years.

TREAT YOURSELF: To one of the Routes des Peintres tours organised by the Caisse Nationale des Monuments Historiques, taking in the art and landscapes that inspired the colourful Pont-Aven school associated with Paul Gaugin. Details from the Office de Tourisme, 5 place de l'Hôtel de Ville, Pont-Aven (00 33 2 98 06 04 70).

GETTING THERE: The campsite is well signposted. From Quimperlé, take the D22 and pass through the village of Arzano before turning left on the D222 to Guilligomarc'h. Come off the D222 and through the village and follow the signposts for the site onto a minor road. The campsite is on the right, shortly before the road rejoins the D222.

OPEN: June–early Sept.

IF IT'S FULL: Nearby, Le Ty-Nadan (Route d'Arzano, 29310 Locunolé; 00 33 2 98 71 75 47; www.camping-ty-nadan.fr) in a quiet river valley, is popular as a watersports venue.

Bois des Écureuils, 29300 Guilligomarc'h | t | 00 33 2 98 71 70 98 | w | www.bois-des-ecureuils.com

château du deffay

Sitting between the estuaries of the Loire and Vilaine rivers, the Parc Naturel Régional de Brière is a monstrous expanse of marsh that resulted from the sea's incursion 7500 years ago, much to the surprise of the Neolithic residents. For collectors of marshy statistics, at nearly 100,000 acres, it's the second largest in France – a vast flatland of reeds and bulrushes crisscrossed by narrow waterways, whose fringes are guarded by megaliths.

The landscape hereabouts can look like a Van Gogh reworking of a classic Constable scene. Slashes of gold and green in the watermeadows, blues and purples across the sky and thin yellow church spires rising from the isolated *îles*. When the wind blows, the reeds seem to move like schools of fish. And the land is as flat as the proverbial Shrove Tuesday treat, sprinkled with lemon and sugar.

The *îles* that poke up here and there in the marsh were once accessible only by boats, which used to punt the thin canals that run roughly north–south and east–west across the place. Now, luckily, there are roads to allow easier access. You'll want to explore the whitewashed cottages with thatched roofs that form these isolated village communities, perched precariously on their little footholds in the marsh. The best of these, Île de Fedrun, looks grandly westwards across La Grande Brière and is a perfect spot to watch the birdies.

If you're a closet twitcher, you can also be poled along the waterways in a punt to get a closer look. Common sights include Cetti's warblers, black-winged stilts and marsh harriers, while with a bit more luck you might spot the odd whiskered tern, whimbrel or spoonbill (charmingly known in French as *la spatule blanche*). Back on dry (well, soggy) land, you can check out the local crafts, all of which are based on the natural environment of the marsh, such as cutting peat, basket weaving, using reeds for thatch and fishing for eels.

And, if you tire of the marshes you can always head to the coast and the beautiful bay at La Baule. Twinned with Inverness in Scotland, the town has the longest sandy beach in Europe – allegedly. It's 7½ miles (12 km) long in any case, to save you strapping a pedometer to your wellies and measuring it yourself.

Luckily you won't need the wellies at Château de Deffay, just outside the village of Sainte-Reine de Bretagne. The campsite is on firmer ground at the edge of this great sea of marsh and reed. The trees are better anchored in the firmer soil and provide shadowy cover for the pitches. In the early morning, whilst the dew's still wet on the ground, you can look out from the snug warmth of your sleeping bag to see the dawn rays of the rising sun slash through the trees, casting long streaks of dark shadow across the grass.

The generous pitches are well spaced and marked out by shrubs and trees. Choose a lakeside spot or settle amongst the chestnut trees. And once you've pitched your tent, take a stroll over the road into the grounds of the *château*. Like Le Brévedent (see p22), it is owned by another ancient aristocratic family, the Espivent de la Villesboisnet, and it oozes class. Or perhaps, given the boggy nature of the surroundings, you should say it squelches class.

THE UPSIDE: Tranquil trees and a grand *château* in a mesmerising natural environment.

THE DOWNSIDE: There are quite a few chalets on the site, though they are mainly on the far side of the lake.

THE DAMAGE: Ranges from €3.20 to €5.10 per adult and €2.15 to €3.50 per child per night, plus €7.60 to €11.60 for a pitch depending on the season. Electricity is €3–4. Two-person chalets are €120–359 a week.

THE FACILITIES: Plenty of toilets and showers for both sexes and good washing-up facilities as well as washing machines. There's a small, sanded play area for children with the usual playground furniture. By the entrance there's a large trampoline, safely caged, and an indoor heated swimming pool.

FOOD AND DRINK: There is a bar/restaurant at the *château*, an Intermarché at Pontchâteau and a well-stocked little *épicerie* in Crossac called La Cuisine aux Beurres for fresh fruit and veg.

FAMILY FUN: Go to the submarine base at the port in Saint-Nazaire (00 33 8 10 88 84 44 for information). This brutalist concrete monstrosity was built after the US Air Force paid a visit during the war and rudely destroyed the old one. The roof of the base is open to the public and is a concrete maze, ideal for playing hide-and-seek. It also has great views from the viewing platforms.

TREAT YOURSELF: To a spectacular multi-course meal at Eric Guerin's wondrous La Mare aux Oiseaux at 162 Île de Fedrun (00 33 2 40 88 53 01; www.mareauxoiseaux.fr). Try to get a table out the back overlooking the garden; if not, enjoy the dining room's mix of bordello and birdhouse. For an aperitif, sample the Pommeau de Bretagne – a soothing brew of cider and calvados. All in all a marvellous experience.

GETTING THERE: Roughly mid-way along the N165 between Vannes and Nantes, come off the autoroute at Pontchâteau and follow the D33 towards Sainte-Reine de Bretagne. About 3 miles (5 km) from the town you'll see Château du Deffay signposted to the right. Follow the road down past the lake and the site entrance is on your left as you climb the hill.

OPEN: May–Sept.

IF IT'S FULL: There are numerous good places to stay at Herbignac and Assérac, closer to the coast, including *aire naturelle* sites (that's rustic), such as La Ferme de Pen-Be (Route de l'Estran, 44410 Assérac; 00 33 2 40 01 78 30).

Camping Château du Deffay, Sainte-Reine de Bretagne, 44160 Pontchâteau

t 00 33 2 40 88 00 57 w www.camping-le-deffay.com

les tipis du bonheur de vivre

There's more to this place than just a tipi over your *tête*. The theme is the philosophy of the Sioux Indians and you'll feel all around you the brooding presence of the great warrior Sitting Bull (Tatanka Iyotaka to his friends) who famously led the Dakota Sioux against General Custer at the Battle of Little Bighorn in 1876.

What's this got to do with camping in rural France? You may well ask. But Les Tipis du Bonheur de Vivre (that's Tipis of Life's Good Fortune) takes its Amerindian philosophy pretty seriously and offers more than just a bit of fun. Sure, you can have a go at bows and arrows and the art of throwing a tomahawk, try tanning hides or just go fishing. But after a hard day of playing Tonto, you can sit in the 'sweat box' – a personal sauna in a tiny hut covered in fir branches – and mull over the natural and environmentally friendly philosophy of the Sioux Indians.

Tipis are available by the night or by the week and can include meals and activities if you fancy the complete Sioux experience. Plans are afoot to move the tipis from their existing site in the small village of Maigné to a far larger site 11 miles (18 km) west in the town of Brûlon, and whilst we're expecting the same set-up in a more spacious location, it's also a good excuse for us to return here soon to check it out.

THE UPSIDE: A truly unique experience.

THE DOWNSIDE: It's rather incongruous in rural France and, let's be honest, a little cheesy.

THE DAMAGE: A 1–3-person tipi costs €50 per night/€290 per week and a 4–6-person tipi is €68/€380 per week. Breakfast is available from €4 per person. If you want to go full-on Hiawatha, then opt for a special 'Amerindian Weekend', available for €119 per person for a group of up to 4 adults or €114 per person for a group between 4 and 8 adults.

THE FACILITIES: By definition, the facilities at the new site will be, well,…new.

FOOD AND DRINK: If you want a night off being camp chef, you can get meals at the site. Otherwise there's not much to shout about gastronomically speaking in Brûlon itself apart from the usual range of *boulangerie*, *pâtisserie*, etc.

FAMILY FUN: As well as the Sioux element, the site organises climbing, tennis, canoeing and kayaking as well as a variety of local excursions.

TREAT YOURSELF: To an afternoon detox in the fir-covered sweatbox.

GETTING THERE: Take the A81 east from Le Mans and exit at junction 1 for Brûlon on the D4. Follow the road into town and follow the signs.

PUBLIC TRANSPORT: The site operates a shuttle bus from the train station at Le Mans to the tipis, leaving the station at noon on a Saturday and returning on Sunday evening. It costs €7 per person each way.

OPEN: Mid-Apr–mid-Oct.

IF IT'S FULL: There's a decent site with a pool by the lake just outside Brûlon. Camping Le Septentrion (Le Lac, 72350 Brûlon; 00 33 2 43 95 68 96; www.campingleseptentrion.com).

Les Tipis du Bonheur de Vivre, Le Plan d'Eau, 72350 Brûlon	t	00 33 6 62 58 66 82	w	www.lebonheurdevivre.net

CAPITAINE

kota cabana

The dilemma: what to do with two ancient sequoia trees and a Lebanese cedar, helpfully planted at the corners of an equilateral triangle in the gardens of a Second Empire *château* near Le Mans? To retired French businessman, Jean-Claude Guillou, already running an exquisite three-bedroomed guest house at the 19th-century Château de l'Enclos in Brûlon, the answer was not immediately obvious. But when a Finnish visitor told him about Lapland *kotas* – wooden dwellings used for everything from fish smokeries to saunas – Jean-Claude had an idea. Why not build a tree house on a platform nestled in the comfortable lap of the branches of his sequoias and cedar? And, not just any old tree house but a mixture of Scandanavian design and French *élan* (with a borrowed touch of Brazilian beach life) – a Kota Cabana.

The resulting structure, high up in the trees, is a largish deck with cosy accommodation for two. Behind the hobbit-like front door, you'll find an octagonal room with a large double bed, a small breakfast table and a couple of easy chairs. A small toilet is tucked discreetly in the corner. The whole cabana is constructed from untreated pine, the smell of whose natural resins permeates the room. It's a magical place and not the kind of camping you may be used to.

Outside on the deck are two seating areas. One is a snug by the branches of the cedar, just above the nest of a neighbouring pigeon, and perfect for settling down with a book; while the other is another breakfast table, overlooking the front of the house. And just about within arm's length is the Captain's bell for summoning room service. Well, you wouldn't want to have to climb down every time you needed some fresh ice to keep the champagne cool, would you? To make things easier still, there's a pulley system for you to haul up the goodies. So, you'll barely need to move from the comfort of your eyrie for the duration of your high-rise stay. There's even a small telescope attached to the railing to zoom in on the local wildlife or just watch the clouds up close.

But if you can be bothered to get out of your tree, take a tour along the valley of the River Sarthe, starting at Spay, where there's a church dating back to the 9th century, and wind along the course of the river through La Suze, Noyen and Solesmes, site of a famous Benedictine abbey, and end up at Sablé where the Rivers Vaige and Erve join the Sarthe. The *château* here is where the French National Library has its book-binding and restoration workshops but if you're not a bibliophile then the town is also famous for its shortbread biscuits or *sablés*. Don't feel guilty about indulging yourself – you'll work off the calories climbing the stairs back at Kota Cabana.

Jean-Claude speaks fluent English (as does his wife, Annie-Claude, who used to teach it) and he is endlessly enthusiastic about his guests: welcoming them into his home like family, showing them the wine cellar, the 1933 burgundy Citroën sitting on the gravel outside, and his goats, donkeys and chickens wandering in the garden. From up in the trees, you'll be able to enjoy the view of the grounds of the *château* stretching away before you and across the valley. Just don't be too put off by the sight in the foreground of two cavorting llamas – they're all just part of the rather unusual world of the Kota Cabana.

THE UPSIDE: Something unique, carried off with tremendous style. Oh, and the *château* does have its own helipad.

THE DOWNSIDE: As there is only the one Kota Cabana and it only sleeps 2 at a time, it is essential to book well in advance.

THE DAMAGE: €130 per night.

THE FACILITIES: There is a toilet and basin in the cabana but the shower is in an annexe next to the house.

FOOD AND DRINK: There's not that much to boast about in Brûlon itself but ring the Captain's bell and order some pulley service.

FAMILY FUN: The cabana gives you the perfect excuse to leave the kids with your parents. Mind you, it's a romantic little place, popular with honeymooners, and as Jean-Claude jokes – 'sometimes they go up two…but they come down three'.

TREAT YOURSELF: To a visit to the 24-hour circuit of Le Mans; a must for all petrolheads. Brûlon is only 20 miles (32 km) along the A81 from Le Mans. The Musée de l'Automobile de la Sarthe (Circuit des 24 Heures du Mans, 72009 Le Mans; 00 33 2 43 72 72 24; www.museeauto24h.sarthe.com) has a selection of cars from the 24-hour race, including a 1924 Bentley and a 1949 Ferrari.

GETTING THERE: Take the A81 from Le Mans and come off at Junction 1 onto the D4 for Brûlon. Follow the road through the town and up the hill and the entrance to Château de l'Enclos is on your right just before you leave the town.

OPEN: The cabana is fully heated and is available all year round.

IF IT'S FULL: There's always the *Cool Camping* site of Les Tipis du Bonheur du Vivre (see p40) nearby or there's a site with a pool by the lake just outside Brûlon. Camping Le Septentrion (Le Lac, 72350 Brûlon; 00 33 2 43 95 68; www.campingleseptentrion.com). Alternatively, there are the three guest rooms in the main house, for €90 per night including breakfast.

Kota Cabana at Château de l'Enclos, 2 avenue de la Libération, 72350 Brûlon

t 00 33 2 43 92 17 85 w www.chateau-enclos.com

L'ESPÉRANCE
RÉMALARD
4K4
DORCEAU
2K8
BRETONCELLES
4K9
LA LOUPE
15K9

forest view

The Parc Naturel Régional du Perche, with its woods of tamarisk and hawthorn (familiar to readers of Proust), is home to the appropriately named Forest View. Run by Yorkshire exiles Pete and Karen Wilson, the site sits by a quiet crossroads between the edge of the Forêt de Saussay and acres of rolling farmland between the towns of Bretoncelles and Rémalard.

It's a very tranquil spot, with the best of the pitches set around a lake, which is stocked with such exotica as roach, rudd and tench. There's a large open orchard area around the back of the farmhouse if you want to spread out and relax with a cool bottle of the local cider from L'Hermitière.

Nearby is the beautiful village of Villeray with a racing water mill, a *château* on the hill, hidden in the trees, and a quiet and unspoilt demeanour that is serenity itself. The restaurant within the old mill is a must, even if it is just for coffee and a croissant – it is fairly expensive.

A little further afield, all you lovers of Proust's *Remembrance of Things Past* will also find the village of Combray, where – depending on whether you're feeling bourgeois or aristocratic – you can follow in the literary footsteps along either Swann's Way or the Guermantes' Way, inhaling the scent of hawthorn as you go.

THE UPSIDE: Small, quiet and friendly site with a tranquil fishing pond and bountiful apple trees.

THE DOWNSIDE: If you can't get a pitch around the lake, the orchard is a bit plain.

THE DAMAGE: €8.50 for a tent/€11.50 for a 4-berth caravan (including electricity), rising to €13 and €16 respectively in July and August.

THE FACILITIES: Fairly rustic. A couple of toilets, a couple of hot showers and a couple of washing-up sinks.

FOOD AND DRINK: There are local markets in Bretoncelles and Rémalard on various days of the week. For some tasty seafood, head for the intimate and friendly Le Galion in Rémalard (21 rue de l'Église; 00 33 2 33 73 81 77).

FAMILY FUN: Try putting your way around the crazy golf course across the road from the campsite. You can borrow a putter from the house. It costs €3 per adult and €2 per child.

TREAT YOURSELF: To the stunning hotel-restaurant Domaine de Villeray (00 33 2 33 73 30 22; www.domainedevilleray.com), an estate with winter dining in the *château* and summer dining in the old water mill. The restaurant, set inside the old timbered mill room, is fabulous and serves superb French cuisine. There's a range of set *menus* from €28 to €69 with anything from three or four to six or seven courses. Expensive yes, but *ooh là là*...

GETTING THERE: Take the N12 from Paris. Just past Dreux bear left onto the D828 and then take the D928 heading for Nogent-le-Rotrou. Approximately 6 miles (9.6 km) after passing through La Loupe, turn right onto the D620 to Bretoncelles. Turn left at Bretoncelles and then right onto the D38 signposted for Rémalard. Just as you reach L'Espérance (which is nothing more than a crossroads) Forest View is on your right, just before the junction.

OPEN: All year.

IF IT'S FULL: This is a relatively remote area but there is a decent thirty-pitch municipal site at nearby Nogent-le-Rotrou. Camping Municipal des Viennes (rue des Viennes, 28400 Nogent-le-Rotrou; 00 33 2 37 52 80 51). There's also a B&B option (three rooms) at the farmhouse for €35 for the bed and €5 for the breakfast. They also rent out a three-bedroom *gîte* for between €325 and €530 per week, depending on the season.

Forest View, L'Espérance, 61110 Dorceau	t	00 33 2 33 25 45 27	w	www.forestviewleisurebreaks.co.uk

huttopia versailles

Sir Thomas More's 1516 treatise on the ideal society, *Utopia*, may seem an unlikely basis for a corporate camping set-up. But that is exactly what the owners of this site of tents, *roulottes* (old-fashioned gypsy caravans) and huts claim – a little hut Utopia. Hence Huttopia. Get it? Never mind – it sounds much better in French anyway.

The company takes a philosophical approach to camping that harks back to a simpler time when people lived in harmony with their natural surroundings. Of course, few people nowadays will be familiar with the work of Sir Thomas More but think of Al Gore in a doublet and hose and you'll get the picture.

The idea is to provide an authentic natural environment, as little altered by human hands as possible – no clearing of trees, levelling the ground or landscaping the gardens. The result is just a naturally contoured patch of forest on the periphery of Paris, up on a hill at the edge of the wood by Viroflay.

The beautifully designed huts at Huttopia are actually quite spacious *cabanes*, sleeping up to six people. The *roulottes* are snugger affairs accommodating up to four in a double and a couple of bunks. But if you just can't sleep without the sound of rippling canvas above your head, you can opt for one of the *canadiennes*, the five-person fixed tents available for hire.
Or, naturally, you can bring your own. The company claims that it prioritises canvas campers and restricts the *cabanes* and *roulottes* to no more than 30% of the pitches.

However admirable the approach, though, no ideal society is perfect. Even in More's *Utopia* each household was allowed to keep a couple of slaves (not available here) and in the end, of course, Henry VIII chopped poor Sir Thomas's head off. There are a few compromises with the utopian concept here, too. For a start there's an environmentally unfriendly swimming pool next to the bar-restaurant, though in the heat of a Parisian summer it's a luxury only the most puritanical environmentalist would shun. And then there's the slightly 'corporate' air that pervades the place. You'll be conscious that the staff – young, enthusiastic and friendly though they are – are employees of a large company rather than owners running their own site.

Putting such minor quibbles aside, though, it all works surprisingly well and there's no doubt that this is a fantastic site. It certainly makes for a different take on a

weekend trip to Paris. It's only 20 minutes by train from the centre of the city and a mere 20 minutes' walk from the palace at Versailles, which is well worth a visit. Any indignation you may have felt about all the water used for the swimming pool might be transformed into burning self-righteousness at the sight of all the fountains, sprinklers and sculpted lakes in the palace gardens. Such beauty just isn't natural, you might say. Yes – but just look around you. These are probably the most stunning gardens in the world. And somewhere between the unspoilt nature at Huttopia and the manipulated perfection at Versailles is, after all, where most of us are content to live.

THE UPSIDE: A real attempt to promote a philosophy of minimal interference with nature.

THE DOWNSIDE: Its proximity to Paris means that it attracts an unwelcome share of beer and BBQ Brits looking for a cheaper option than a budget hotel in the capital. As a result, the camping area can be quite noisy late into the night.

THE DAMAGE: High season (July and August) it's €13.90 for a tent plus €7.90 per adult and €4 for a child (2–7 years). Low season, prices dip to €10 for a tent plus €6 per adult and €3 for a child. Electricity ranges from €4 to €6.20 depending on season and ampage. *Cabanes, roulottes* and *canadiennes* are available only for a minimum of 2 nights and range from €55 to €159 per night.

THE FACILITIES: Three substantial blocks of clean, well-maintained facilities. There are open air urinals (men only!) and plenty of toilets, plus dishes and deep clothes-washing sinks. There's also a free Internet terminal in reception.

FOOD AND DRINK: There's a bar and restaurant next to the pool serving reasonable but not exciting pizzas, steaks, salads and beers. But this is Paris (well, almost), so there are gastronomic delights aplenty just a short train ride away.

FAMILY FUN: Though the gardens at Versailles are free to enter, it is worth paying €13.50 (€10 after 4pm) to tour the palace itself and even to pay an extra €7 to see the Grandes Eaux Musicales when the fountains are turned on and choreographed to music. This only happens at weekends, however, and it's best to see it at night.

TREAT YOURSELF: To a copy of Sir Thomas More's *Utopia*, available from all good bookshops.

GETTING THERE: Avoid Paris's *périphérique* (ring road) if you can. Head away from the Palace of Versailles along the broad avenue de Paris. After it bends left, there are two sandstone gatehouses on either side of the road. Turn right here onto avenue de Porchefontaine. Go under the railway line and carry on along rue Costa until you hit rue Rémont. Turn left and then right onto rue Berthelot. Huttopia is at the top of the road on the left.

PUBLIC TRANSPORT: The RER C regional train station of Porchefontaine is a few minutes' walk from the site. Frequent trains to and from Paris take approximately 20 minutes. There is also a B-line bus stop on rue Yves Le Coz at the bottom of rue Berthelot, which goes to and from the Palace of Versailles and a bus No. 171 from avenue de Paris about five minutes' extra walk.

OPEN: Late-Mar–Nov.

IF IT'S FULL: There is another Huttopia site at Rambouillet (Route du Château d'Eau, 78120 Rambouillet; 00 33 1 30 41 07 34).

Huttopia Versailles, 31 rue Berthelot, 78000 Versailles	t	00 33 1 39 51 23 61	w	www.huttopia.com

RUE
MOLÉ

camping de troyes

There's something apposite about the medieval town of Troyes – the capital of the Champagne region – having a town centre that's shaped like a champagne cork. It's a lovely centre, too: a huddle of medieval buildings that stand out proudly against the town's work-a-day charm. Though formed in the Roman era, most of Troyes' architecture dates from the Middle Ages when it was an important trading town.

Just along the road, in Pont-Sainte-Marie, is Camping de Troyes, the town's official campsite. Though a former municipal spot, owners Dirk, Marie and their Irish friend Bill have done everything in their power to transform it into something much more alluring than the word 'municipal' suggests.

This green and peaceful site has 110 spots open to tents and caravans; there are 20 tent-only pitches. Amenities are decent and include a modern, heated sanitary block, playground, on-site restaurant and well-stocked shop that sells everything from wine and rice to pasta and plasters.

Those not wanting to explore the town can busy themselves with the nearby Parc Naturel Régional de la Forêt d'Orient, just 20 minutes away by car. The forest's natural lakes proffer plenty of outdoor activities and can be accessed by La vélovoie verte (Green Bicycle Path) – detailed maps are available at reception.

THE UPSIDE: Municipal camping the way it should be – very un-municipal!

THE DOWNSIDE: Although it doesn't feel it, Camping de Troyes is a fairly large site (110 pitches) and may not hit the spot for those wanting an intimate camping experience.

THE DAMAGE: Two people with vehicle and tent is €14.70 per night. An additional adult (12 or older) is €4.40 and children (2–11) are €3.

THE FACILITIES: There are plenty of decent facilities on site. The toilet and shower block are modern and clean, and there's plenty of free, on-site stuff for kids to do.

FOOD AND DRINK: Wop Wop, the on-site restaurant, sells salads, pizzas and steaks. Bistro du Pont, 300 m along the road, sells good local dishes at reasonable prices. Foodies should stroll a little further to the town's Michelin-starred spot, Hostellerie de Pont-Sainte-Marie (34 rue Pasteur, Pont-Sainte-Marie; 00 33 3 25 83 28 61). Troyes' daily market has a local products and food bias on Saturdays.

FAMILY FUN: The site's dedicated playground and air-trampoline tends to keep kids bouncingly happy.

TREAT YOURSELF: To a spot of hot-air ballooning; ask at reception for details.

GETTING THERE: The site is actually in Pont-Sainte-Marie, rather than Troyes, though Troyes is the nearest main town. You can get to Troyes by six main roads: N19, N60, N71, N77, D960 and the D444. Follow the directions for Troyes then Pont-Sainte-Marie and then follow the 'municipal camping' signs.

PUBLIC TRANSPORT: Troyes is easily reached by train or bus from most major French towns. A bus service runs from the centre to within 50 m of the site (and back).

OPEN: Apr–mid-Oct.

IF IT'S FULL: There's nothing else nearby with the same kind of easy charm as Camping de Troyes, but Camping L'Épine aux Moines (Plage de Géraudot, 10220 Géraudot; 00 33 3 25 41 24 36) is a decent alternative.

Camping de Troyes, 7 Rue Roger Salengro, 10150 Pont-Sainte-Marie

t 00 33 3 25 81 02 64 w www.troyescamping.net

les grèbes du lac de marcenay

As lakes go, Marcenay's has some pretty varied history. It was once tended by medieval monks (who plucked their Friday fish supper from it), has been used to power a water tower for steel-making and now makes for a sparklingly beautiful tourist attraction. What's more, there's a campsite just on the shore that could form your perfect little lakeside retreat.

Visitors today come to Lac de Marcenay to loll about on its natural beach, to picnic on its shore and to scoot across its glittering surface in pedalos and kayaks.

Les Grèbes du Lac de Marcenay was given a new lease of life a couple of years ago by Dirk Jansen and his partner Marie Albaret. If you think those names are familiar then it's the same Dutch–French couple that injected some life and soul into another *Cool Camping* site – Camping de Troyes (see p54). They've applied a similar laid-back philosophy here with equally pleasant results, perhaps even more so, given the bucolic nature of the area.

The site's 90 pitches are arranged in small clearings separated by shrubs and hedges. Whilst none of the pitches backs right onto the lake (the site has to be fenced off for legal reasons; shame!), some of them do offer lake views.

Dirk and Marie have been busy making the site as attractive and welcoming as possible; planting extra trees and flowers, getting everything neat and sweet, and creating a reception area that's satisfyingly stylish and brimming with activities. Aside from the shop and snack bar there's a small library with sofas and chairs to relax or read on, plus a pool table and kids' games.

If you're coming *en famille*, then the campsite is well set up. Not only is the lake right next door, there's a zoo near Montbard (half an hour's drive), a local theme park and a delightful deer park at Châteauvillain. And for watery fun and games, you can borrow the site's canoes and rowing boats.

There isn't a restaurant on site but a few metres down the road is a decent, inexpensive restaurant that also hires bikes. A favourite pastime here – aside from lake-based activities – is to walk and cycle through the forests and vineyards of the area. Arc-en Barrois and Châtillon-sur-Seine are easily accessible and fun to explore. The former boasts a large forest with traffic-free tracks, as well as a public tennis court, golf course and you can even hire horses; whilst Châtillon's museum (located in an opulent Renaissance house) displays the fascinating Etruscan booty 'Trésor de Vix'.

If you fancy a day out and change of scene, then just a little further away are several other significant towns and sights: Autun and its 12th-century cathedral, the medieval town of Beaune, Cluny (Europe's largest Benedictine abbey), Dijon's Palace of the Dukes and – last but certainly not least – Fontenay Abbey, one of the oldest Cistercian monasteries in France and a UNESCO World Heritage Site.

Foodies might want to try local dishes like *poulet au Meursault* (chicken cooked in a local Meusault white wine), *coq au Chambertin* (a chicken stew using Napoléon's alleged favourite burgundy, a Gevrey-Chambertin red), *boeuf Bourguignon* (we all know what this is) and specialities like *gougère Bourgignon* (a cheesy pastry stuffed with Gruyère) and *jambon persillé* (parsley-flavoured ham, served cold in jelly). If you can't locate them, don't worry. There's always the opportunity to catch your own supper in the lake and slap it on the BBQ back at the ranch.

THE UPSIDE: Peace and quiet next to a fabulous lake.

THE DOWNSIDE: You can't actually pitch lakeside.

THE DAMAGE: For 2 people and a tent it's €12.50; 4 people and a tent costs €19.50.

THE FACILITIES: The main reception area is new and very smart, and boasts table football, board games and a pool table. The showers are good, and there's electricity and chemical disposal. You can have fires and BBQs as long as they're off the ground. The site aims to have wi-fi from 2008.

FOOD AND DRINK: The best local spot, Restaurant Le Santenoy (00 33 3 80 81 40 08) is right on the lake, strolling distance from the site. It serves up regional specialties and traditional cooking on two floors; a panoramic dining room that overlooks the lake and a ground floor that acts as bar, grill and large summer terrace. For an exploration of local recipes and foods, try nearby Maison du Terroir (00 33 3 80 81 14 14; ask at reception for directions). You can even buy flour produced by local mills at Moulin Maurice (00 33 3 80 93 20 49; www.moulin-maurice.com).

FAMILY FUN: The lake provides many watersport options, which can be easily organised via the campsite (they have free rowing boats) and there are lifeguards in the summer. There's also plenty of cycling and hiking in the area. And there's always the Nigloland theme park (00 33 3 25 27 94 52; www.nigloland.fr).

TREAT YOURSELF: To a stay at a quintessentially romantic 15th-century house, in the lovely town of Troyes (1 hour away by car). Le Champ des Oiseaux (20 rue Linard Gonthier; 00 33 3 25 80 58 50; www.champdesoiseaux.com) is perfect.

GETTING THERE: The site is on the D965 between Laignes and Châtillon-sur-Seine. Follow signposts to Lac de Marcenay and 'Camping'.

PUBLIC TRANSPORT: There's a train station (TGV) at Montbard, which is 30 minutes south of the site. You can catch a bus from Montbard to Châtillon-sur-Seine and then onwards from there on one of the buses from Châtillon-sur-Seine to Marcenay; although the last stretch may well be quicker by taxi.

OPEN: May–Sept.

IF IT'S FULL: Camping Louis Rigoly (esplanade Saint-Vorles, 21400 Châtillon-sur-Seine; 00 33 3 80 91 03 05) is 6 miles (10 km) away, has 54 pitches and is next to the public swimming pool.

Les Grèbes du Lac de Marcenay, 5 Route du Lac, Marcenay, 21330 Marcenay

t 00 33 3 80 81 61 72 w www.campingmarcenaylac.com

101 Å 105
122 A 123

domaine du haut des bluches

Surrounded by the stunning Vosges mountains, with their rounded *ballons* (summits), and set in a natural location close to forests and rivers, Domaine du Haut des Bluches – which stands at an altitude of 710 metres – is an excellent campsite spot for gurus of the Great Outdoors.

Though at first glance a large and fairly commercial site (140 pitches), the owners work hard to create an intimate and friendly character, and to make the most of the site's unsurpassed access to the mountains and surrounding landscape.

Nearby La Bresse (4 km away) is well known as a winter-sport resort, though what's not so well promoted is the fact that it also has over 180 miles (300 km) of marked walking and cycling paths and plenty of activities (horse riding, bicycle hire, fishing and golf), making it a solid summer option, too. There's plenty for kids to do here: a swimming pool and leisure complex, ice-skating rink and an adventure park.

Mums and dads meanwhile may be interested to know that Lorraine – the region, not the girl from the Campari ad – is more about beer than wine and even has an official 'Beer Route', offering such enticing sights as the Musée Européen de la Bière in Stenay (10 rue de la Citadelle, Stenay; 00 33 3 29 80 68 78; www.musee-de-la-biere.com) – the biggest beer museum in the world. Cheers!

THE UPSIDE: Family-friendly campsite with good amenities and great access to the mountains.

THE DOWNSIDE: Commercial site with quite a few statics.

THE DAMAGE: Two people plus tent and car costs €12. Additional adults are €2.60 and children (13 and under) €0.95.

THE FACILITIES: The site has full facilities, including a restaurant and snack bar, a games room and outdoor playground.

FOOD AND DRINK: The campsite's restaurant has a reasonable set menu that sometimes has local dishes like Quiche Lorraine and *les toffailles* (potatoes, onions, smoked meat and salad). In the summer, the market in La Bresse on a Sunday sells local produce and there are lots of *fermes auberges* (farms that double up as restaurants and serve mostly homegrown or local products) both in La Bresse and in the mountains.

FAMILY FUN: For all-year-round action, there's a climbing wall in the leisure complex at La Bresse (00 33 3 29 25 41 29; www.labresse.net). Ski lessons are available (winter-only) in La Bresse (www.labresse.net) as well as an ice rink and an adventure park.

TREAT YOURSELF: To a hang-gliding lesson, just 500 metres from the campsite. Ask at reception.

GETTING THERE: Take the D34 in the direction of Col de la Schlucht and Colmar. Two and a half miles (4 km) from the village you will see Route des Planches on the right.

PUBLIC TRANSPORT: You can get a train to Remiremont, then a bus to La Bresse. From La Bresse the site is 2½ miles (4 km) (taxi only).

OPEN: Almost all year (closed Nov–mid-Dec).

IF IT'S FULL: Camping de Belle-Hutte (88250 La Bresse; 00 33 3 29 25 49 75; www.camping-belle-hutte.com) is 3 miles (5 km) away. It's a pleasant, family-run site also with good access to the Vosges.

Domaine du Haut des Bluches, 5 Route des Planches, 88250 La Bresse

t 00 33 3 29 25 64 80 | w www.domainehautdesbluches.labresse.fr

le grand champ

In the foothills of the legendary Mont Blanc mountain range, directly beneath the towering peak of Aiguille du Midi, you'll find Camping Le Grand Champ – and what a find. Run by Françoise Dudas and her family, the site is in a tip-top location, 1000 metres up in the sky, with mountain views wherever you look.

The jagged and oft-snow-topped blocks of rock that dominate the horizon in every direction, make this place feel like a secret valley, cut off from the world and stranded in happy seclusion. And whilst the spike-strewn view is the most obvious of the sites charms, there are plenty of other reasons to recommend Le Grand Champ as one of the most appealing of Alpine camps.

The beautiful terraced garden boasts pretty pitches, all grassy and green, and separated by a neat but natural jumble of trees, bushes and hedges. Even though there's room for up to 100 tents or caravans, you'd never guess, since the layout of the gardens lends a very intimate feel. Whilst groups are welcome, they are directed to a separate area, ensuring peace and privacy at all times for the other tenters.

Françoise and the gang do everything in their power to make sure the site functions perfectly. The facilities are in decent shape, with three sanitary blocks (sinks and showers, hot and cold water), access for disabled visitors, washing machines and electricity; there's even a basic but cosy little communal room. And if you're running low on supplies, just pop along to the reception, where you'll find a few essentials on sale. Fresh bread is delivered every day during the summer months, just in time for breakfast.

The nearest supermarket is in the town of Les Houches, almost 2 miles (3 km) along the road. Comprised of a number of hamlets, Les Houches has a certain alpine charm, as well as great ski slopes, a lake and castle ruins. Climbing fans will enjoy the town's indoor wall, whilst walkers can begin the Tour du Mont-Blanc there.

Nearby, Chamonix is a far cry from the peace and tranquillity of the site – but, it's a bit of a mixed blessing. With its myriad cafés, restaurants, tourist facilities and activity centres, it makes a fantastic hub for anyone wanting to explore the region. But (and you knew there was a 'but' coming), with up to 40,000 people a day in the surrounding valley during peak season, it has a resort atmosphere that erodes its more natural charms.

METEO

Although this area is best known for its ski slopes, it offers something for every kind of thrill-seeker. In fact, it would be easier to list what it doesn't have: you can hike, cycle, climb, raft, kart, golf, abseil, glide, swim, snowboard – and that's just for starters. *Entrées* could include canyoning, hot-air ballooning, paintballing and off-road mountain biking. And, why not round the menu off with a sedate ride in a helicopter, horse trek or a game of *boules*?

And if you should tire of all the activities and feel in need of a well-earned rest, then Chamonix offers the opportunity to be indulgent as well as active. There can't be many campsites in the midst of a natural wonderland that also offer cinemas, beauty salons, casinos and shopping so close by.

At the end of the day, just zip up the tent flaps on that vertiginous view, snuggle into your sleeping back and join Le Grand Champ's version of the mile-high club – snoozing at altitude in this freshest of mountain air.

THE UPSIDE: Drop-dead gorgeous site on the doorstep of Mont Blanc.

THE DOWNSIDE: Self-sufficiency is the name of the game here, as there's not much except the supermarket within walking distance.

THE DAMAGE: It's €4.30 for a pitch, €4.50 per adult and €2.20 per child (under 7).

THE FACILITIES: The facilities, in keeping with the site, are fairly basic – just a small shop and decent sanitary provisions.

FOOD AND DRINK: Aside from the classic Savoyard specialties (*fondue, raclette, tartiflette* and *farcement*) you can find most kinds of food in this area. A decent local option is the hotel-restaurant Les Gorges de la Diosaz in Servoz (00 33 4 50 47 20 97; www.hoteldesgorges.com), which serves good French dishes and has a great terrace. For something more swish, Les Granges d'en Haut Les Houches (00 33 4 50 91 48 70; www.grangesdenhaut.com) is a contemporary spot above Les Houches with novel twists on French classics and very good brunch options.

FAMILY FUN: There's so much for families here. Options include Les Gaillands in Chamonix, a natural climbing crag great for children and beginners (follow the 'Taconnaz, Bossons' signs from Chamonix, and the wall is on your left, opposite the lake); and a tree-based activity centre (00 33 6 62 67 28 51; www.arbreaventure-montblanc.com).

TREAT YOURSELF: To a romantic dinner at Le Hameau Albert 1er (38 Route du Bouchet, 74402 Chamonix-Mont-Blanc; 00 33 4 50 53 05 09; www.hameaualbert.fr).

GETTING THERE: Les Bossons is located directly off the E25/A40 just over 2 miles (3.5 km) from Chamonix. The site is signposted from the village.

PUBLIC TRANSPORT: Chamonix is accessible by train and bus from most major French towns. From Chamonix, you can catch a bus to the nearby shops, just over half a mile (1 km) away. There's also a railway station at Les Bossons just over a mile (2 km) away.

OPEN: May–mid-Oct.

IF IT'S FULL: Glacier d'Argentière, 161 chemin des Chosalets, 74400 Argentière (00 33 4 50 54 17 36; www.campingchamonix.com) is one of Chamonix's more scenic and *naturelle* campsites.

Camping Le Grand Champ, 167 chemin du Glacier de Taconnaz, Les Bossons, 74400 Chamonix-Mont-Blanc

t 00 33 4 50 53 04 83 e campinggrandchamp@hotmail.com

le prieuré

Warning! Members of the cloud appreciation society should avoid Le Prieuré. Here, you see acres and acres of unblemished blue sky almost every day. Whilst lovers of cumulus might view this as something of a drawback, the rest of us can enjoy the sense of space and freedom it imparts.

Located high up in the French southern Alps, Le Prieuré is an old farm that's been lovingly converted into a campsite. With tent pitches ensconced within an alpine environment that's all slender firs and dramatic mountain peaks, the place oozes tranquillity, yet offers heaps of outdoor action at the same time.

The farm's current owners – Cathy and Gilles (not forgetting Moumoute, the cat) – have been here for around six years. Though large (about 30 acres), the site caters for just 35 tents, as well as six wooden bungalows and 10 *gîtes*, ensuring maximum space and comfort is allocated to all the site's guests.

Scattered around the site is a range of activity possibilities, including a tennis court, solar-heated swimming pool, volleyball court and playground for children. There's also a games and television room, and a library too – but chances are you'll be outside much more than in.

Despite being located at an altitude of 1050 metres above sea level, the mountain climate here is tempered by the Mediterranean coast to give extraordinary good weather – and inordinately blue skies with barely more than a half-hearted cloudy wisp – for much of the year.

The site's proximity to the wonderful Parc National du Mercantour really gives it the edge. The Mercantour is a paradise for hikers, with over 375 miles (600 km) of marked footpaths and a wealth of wildlife including ibexes, chamois, marmots and the like. A local activities company visits Le Prieuré a couple of times a week, and can organise walking, canyoning, climbing, mountain biking or via Ferrata (climbing assisted by ladders and cables) trips.

This being the Alps, there are plenty of skiing options available, too. Local resorts like Valberg and Val Pelens offer decent slopes, cross-country skiing and snow-shoe-walking. Val Pelens is very close by and specialises in children's skiing. Valberg, just 15 miles (24 km) from the site, offers 55 miles (90 km) of downhill skiing, split into descents of around 300–400 metres.

There are plenty of small charming towns in the area, such as nearby Guillaumes, about

7 miles (11 km) away – a mountain market town with a strong Italian character. As well as being a great base for walks to the abandoned villages of Barels or Amen (which has an old copper mine), Guillaumes also has a smattering of amenities – hotels, cafés, restaurants, bakeries and such.

Back at the site, Cathy and Gilles both work hard to make a stay at Le Prieuré highly memorable. As well as welcoming guests, dealing with the administration and taking bookings, Cathy is an enthusiastic maker of picnics, an essential supply for any long days in the mountains (orders to be received a day in advance, ideally). Gilles busies himself with the technical aspects of the site and making sure the pool is always clean and working correctly. And in the winter, he also takes over the farmhouse's rustic kitchen to serve up lovely home-made French food. There's no menu – it all depends on the ingredients available, your preferences and his mood!

When the weather does take a turn and the clumps of cumulus hang like threatening gangs, it's easy enough to catch a bus down to Nice, 60 miles (100 km) away, where you'll find a multitude of sea-level attractions. So, it seems every cloud really does have a silver lining.

THE UPSIDE: You're high up in the southern Alps with the Mercantour National Park at your feet.

THE DOWNSIDE: It can get a little chilly in the evenings outside summer.

THE DAMAGE: A pitch costs between €6.90 and €8.60 depending on the size. Adults pay €4.20, children (under 5) €2.50. Electricity costs are €3 for 3-amps and €4 for 10-amps.

THE FACILITIES: The price of your pitch gives you free access to most of the sports facilities mentioned, though there's a charge for tennis courts in July and August. Shower blocks are modern and clean, and come with hot water and toilet paper. A washing machine is also available.

FOOD AND DRINK: Good meals are available on-site throughout summer (and on demand in winter). A local farm brings a selection of cow's cheese to the site once a week, and honey heads will want to meet Suzanne, a Canadian lady who keeps bees down in Guillaumes. For *foie gras*, truffles and other foodie kicks, try the dependable Le Versus in Annotave du Foulon, Annot (00 33 4 92 83 31 80); it's nearly 30 miles (45 km) away but so mouth-wateringly worth it.

FAMILY FUN: Both of the local ski places offer lessons for children, and Valberg (15 miles/25 km away) also has a luge run (00 33 4 93 23 24 25; www.valberg.com). For something more sedate, go horse riding *en famille* at the local ranch – tours range from 40 minutes to half-days. Ask at reception for details.

TREAT YOURSELF: To a bungee jump for two. Sounds romantic? Head to the Pont de la Mariée at the nearby Gorges de Daluis. Reception can help you book.

GETTING THERE: From Nice or Digne-les-Bains, leave the N202 at the Pont de Gueydan crossing, and take the D2202 to Guillaumes. Saint-Martin-d'Entraunes is located on the DR2202, 7 miles (12 km) north of Guillaumes. Le Prieuré is signposted from Saint-Martin-d'Entraunes.

PUBLIC TRANSPORT: Buses run to Guilluames from Nice daily. There are no buses from Guillaumes to Le Prieuré so make sure you call the site in advance to arrange a pick-up.

OPEN: May–Oct (camping); all year for *gîtes*.

IF IT'S FULL: Camping du Pont de la Mariée in Guillaumes (Quartier de Tire Boeuf, Gorges de Daluis; 00 33 4 93 05 53 50) is a friendly and well-located alternative.

Le Prieuré, Route des Blancs, 06470 Saint-Martin-d'Entraunes	t	00 33 4 93 05 54 99	w	www.le-prieure.com

Quechua

ferme noemie

Perhaps the best way to describe this glorious alpine setting is simply to say that the hills are alive with 'the Sound of Music'. Not real music, of course, but as you take in the soaring peaks and a horizon line that resembles a graph of a turbulent day in the stock market, it's impossible not to start humming something by Julie Andrews. Feel free to whirl around as you sing. It'll give you the chance to have a good look around this stunningly located campsite.

The site's 15 pitches are arranged on a flat area of beautifully manicured grass and gathered around an attractive wooden eco-hut that features the very best kind of sanitary facilities. Think dedicated washing-up sinks, real toilets with posh toilet paper, facilities for people with limited mobility – and all spotlessly clean. Plus all the pitches have hook-ups for electricity and water, if desired.

Owners Jeremy, Mel and Sean have also added some thoughtful extras to help make this site stand out. There's a lovely chill-out area under an apple tree, perfect for lounging around in the shade; a play area including badminton, *boules* and swingball; a large BBQ with picnic benches and tables; first-rate laundry facilities; separate bowls for washing salads; and a bread service in the mornings.

But that's the detail. The big picture is that this site has an outstanding mountain vista, with peaks shooting to the skies all around. This area features some of the most formidable mountains in Europe with the highest peaks reaching over 4000 metres. Add to that a mere 40 square miles (100 sq. km) of glaciers, and you've got some serious high-altitude landscape. Of course, you can't see all this from your tent, but you can see enough to get the urge to 'Climb Every Mountain', so to speak.

It's just a five-minute drive or 10-minute cycle from the campsite to the town of Bourg d'Oisans. The town is full of cyclists and walkers using it as a base for enjoying the alpine Parc National des Écrins, France's largest national park. Despite a high proportion of tourists, it has retained much of its intimate, mountain-town charm and is a picturesque place for a *chocolat chaud* or *crêpe*. The campsite is also just a half-hour drive from the Alpe d'Huez ski resort – where you can even ski in summer – and it's also close to the notorious '21 bends', one of the most challenging stages of the Tour de France. Factor in a nearby 9-hole golf course, horse riding, mountain biking and trout fishing options and a sports centre with indoor and outdoor swimming pools – and you have yourself a one-stop action HQ!

- AOC -
16,50
ABONDANCE
à la Provençale
Sauce Escabèche
Tommette de Brebis
12,00 € la pièce
20,00 € les 2

Aside from the activities and amenities available in Bourg d'Oisans, there are a wealth of other places to explore in the vicinity. Vaujany, a picturesque alpine village has a natural ice rink in winter and beautiful walks. Allemont has a great lake for fishing, windsurfing, sailing, kayaking and pedalos. And Venosc is famous for its white-water rafting.

Since Mel and Jeremy have been working in this region for many years and know it intimately, they're very enthusiastic about supplying all the sightseeing and activities information you'll need to make your visit as memorable and fun as possible.

It's this extra level of service, the attention to detail on-site – and, of course, the memorable landscape around it – that makes this place special. Blame it on the high-altitude confusing your emotions, but after spending time in this unique and lofty spot, anyone would find it difficult to say (or sing) So long. Farewell. Auf weidersehen. Goodbye...

THE UPSIDE: Mountain views to sing about.

THE DOWNSIDE: Limited number of pitches, and a few static caravans spoil the view.

THE DAMAGE: €15–24 per night (depending on season/number of people). Special family rate of €30 per night regardless of number of children (under 15).

THE FACILITIES: The modern, wooden sanitary block includes showers, sinks and washing and drying machines. There's also a well-equipped children's play area, private parking, Internet access, a payphone and a babysitting service.

FOOD AND DRINK: Bourg d'Oisans has several recommended restaurants including La Romanche, which offers a wide selection of local dishes and excellent salads. In Alpe d'Huez, the Edelweiss and the Passe Montagne keep locals and tourists alike fully sated. The Saturday market in Bourg d'Oisans is the place to hang out with true 'Bourcats' (people of Bourg d'Oisans) and shop for cheeses, breads and fresh meats.

FAMILY FUN: Bourg d'Oisans has a good public swimming pool and an excellent pool for toddlers. For the more adventurous, skiing and snowboarding courses/days can easily be arranged in Alpe d'Huez, whilst the village of Allemont has a man-made lake with pedalos, kayaks and windsurfers and fishing.

TREAT YOURSELF: To a tandem hang-gliding trip over the mountains. The tourist office in Bourg d'Oisans is the place to find out more (00 33 4 76 80 03 25; www.bourgdoisans.com).

GETTING THERE: From Grenoble head in the direction of Briançon, Vallée de l'Oisans. Enter Les Sables on the N91, 2 miles (3.5 km) before Bourg d'Oisans. Ferme Noemie is clearly signposted to the right. Airport transfers and private shuttle services to and from local resorts are available for an extra charge (book in advance).

PUBLIC TRANSPORT: Bus transfers to Grenoble bus/train station are available from both Lyon and Grenoble. There are regular bus links to Bourg d'Oisans. A limited service runs between the campsite and Bourg d'Oisans, but bicycles are readily available for the short trip, and pick-ups can also be arranged (call in advance).

OPEN: End-March–end-Oct; all year for apartments.

IF IT'S FULL: Camping Le Colporteur (Le Pré du May, 38520 Bourg d'Oisans; 00 33 4 76 79 11 44; www.camping-colporteur.com) is commercial but well-located and packed with facilities.

Ferme Noemie, chemin Pierre Polycarpe, Les Sables, 38520 Bourg d'Oisans

	t	00 33 4 76 11 06 14	w	www.fermenoemie.com

la source

It has been scientifically proven that the jagged, jaw-dropping mountain vistas common to France's Hautes-Alpes region can move even the most timid and tone-deaf visitor to spontaneous bursts of yodelling. Whilst the Joffan mountain range that provides a backdrop to La Source may not boast the most peaks in the region, they're enough to prompt casual thoughts about lederhosen and singing lessons.

Nestled in the famous Buëch valley, La Sources's *aire-naturelle* ambience, proximity to a broad swathe of peaks and the warm hospitality of the owners conspire to make this one of the most compelling camping spots in the region. Centred around an attractive old farmhouse, the vast undulating grounds of the site are decorated with an array of trees that leave plenty of room to absorb and appreciate the big blue skies and feeling of wide open space.

The site is run by two friendly English couples – Tony and Carol, Robert and Glenda – who came here from Darlington after falling head over heels in love with the farmhouse and the region a few years ago. With just 10 pitches, there's not much chance of your peace and quiet being disturbed – which is just how the owners planned it. There are designated spots – by law there has to be in France – but if it's not busy, you can pretty much set up wherever you like. As long as you're within the campsite grounds and not invading anyone else's personal space, you won't be told off.

The site is fairly minimal in terms of facilities: there are essentials like electric points, constant hot water and showers, as well as pot-washing sinks, washing machines and a communal BBQ. And that's all you're going to need in this area, which is in essence a large adventure playground.

Being slap-bang in the middle of the Hautes-Alpes region, the site is a wonderful choice for outdoors types. You can literally walk and cycle for miles and miles. Multitudinous routes can be accessed directly from La Source, and the surrounding Alps and Buëch valley boast almost 4300 miles (7000 km) of footpaths and trails. You can even join the GR94 national walking route if you want – it passes right by the front door.

Climbers can grapple with crags and vertical walls aplenty at specialist places in the nearby villages of Orpierre and Sigottier. And skiers get an even better deal – there are no less than four ski-slopes in the area (SuperDévoluy, La Joue du Loup, Céüze 2000, La Jarjatte) that provide the region with no end of fun, from cross-country skiing to snowboarding in the winter, to walking, biking and climbing in the summer.

Oh, and if you feel like getting airborne – no problem. There's a hang-gliding take-off point at La Longeagne behind La Source and even an allocated landing field at Saint-Pierre-d'Argençon. Chevalet – a recreational airport – is only 3 miles (5 km) away where you can book glider flights or lessons.

If you need some variety then head to the nearby town of Serres for plenty of cultural and historical distractions, especially in the summer when there are jazz festivals (July) and festivals of light (August), plus lively markets on various mornings. Gap (the village, not the commercial clothing franchise) has a wealth of culture; the worryingly-named village of Die, not a place for Buddhist-style meditations on reincarnation, is a centre for wine and white-water rafting; and if you crave outstanding views, hit the Col du Noyer.

The more enthusiastic can make good use of the many tourist circuits in the area. There's a fruit and wine route, lavender routes, the Napoléon route, an Alpine route and a sundial route – these are all fantastic ways to both keep fit and simultaneously absorb the local culture. At the time of writing, there were no official yodelling schools in the area, but amateur attempts are generally encouraged.

THE UPSIDE: Scenery and serenity in the High Alps.

THE DOWNSIDE: No bars or pubs in the vicinity.

THE DAMAGE: It's €4 per night for a pitch, €2.50 per adult and €1.50 per child (under 7). Electricity costs €2.50 per night.

THE FACILITIES: The toilets (English style!) and showers are in good nick and have constant hot water. There are two washing machines, a communal BBQ and Internet access is possible.

FOOD AND DRINK: The best place to buy regional products like apple and pear juice, *tourtons* (small pastries filled with potato, cheese and onion purée), lavender and honey is at local markets, such as those in Serres and Veynes (it's best to ask at reception for days and times). The closest restaurant is the Auberge de la Tour (05140 Saint-Pierre-d'Argençon; 00 33 4 92 58 71 08), just over 1 mile (2 km) away; a traditional, rustic and reasonably small spot.

FAMILY FUN: Family climbing instruction is available at Orpierre. There are also swimming lakes located at Veynes and Germinette, tennis courts and horse riding at Aspres-sur-Buëch and quad-biking at Serres (reception can help organise any of these activities).

TREAT YOURSELF: To a flying lesson. Check out the pilot school at Alp'Air (00 33 4 92 57 13 06; alp.air.free.fr). Or, if you fancy the wind in your hair but with added water spray, then hit the biggest lake in Europe, the Lac de Serre Ponçon, for some yachting (www.serre-poncon.com).

GETTING THERE: Head south from Lyon and Grenoble, follow signs to Sisteron. Follow the RN75 to Aspres-sur-Buëch. Take the right-hand D993 route to Valence for about 4 miles (7 km). La Source is just after Saint-Pierre-d'Argençon on the right, and is well signposted from Valence.

OPEN: Mid-Apr–mid-Oct.

IF IT'S FULL: Camping L'Adrech in Aspres-sur-Buëch (Route de Sisteron; 00 33 4 92 58 60 45) is a pleasant site with 25 pitches and a pool.

La Source, 05140 Saint-Pierre-d'Argençon | t | 00 33 4 92 58 67 81 | w | www.lasource-hautesalpes.com

les roulottes de la serve

Roulottes – covered gypsy caravans originally designed for nomads – are now officially *en vogue* with campers throughout France. Whilst some sites are content with bunging a few standard-issue caravans in a field and charging a nightly rate, others offer an altogether more distinctive experience.

Les Roulottes de la Serve is one such place: three *roulottes*, tucked away in an Arcadian setting, on a super-rustic farm that's out of the way of everything. Rewind 20 years and owners Pascal (Pat) and Pascaline had some horses that needed a field. They bought a derelict 19th-century farmhouse and devoted their lives to restoring it. And the horses were over the moon – they got much larger fields than they'd hoped for.

Pat and Pascaline were offered their first *roulotte* by a local merry-go-round owner (you couldn't make it up). They put it in the field, alongside the horses, and decided they liked it so much they wanted a couple more. Fast forward 15 or so years and – following an eight-month jaunt through Africa and India – the pair now have three *roulottes* and some seriously good interior décor ideas. *Et voilà!* Les Roulottes de la Serve was born.

The site is beautifully off the beaten track. An engaging climb through the undulating hills of Les Ardillats in the middle of the Beaujolais countryside leads to a narrow country lane and a dense garden of trees, plants and meadows. A wooden cart brimming with apples sits beneath a tree. A huge Saint Bernard dog basks in the golden sunlight. Horses worry gently at lush green grass. It's a painterly *tableau*.

Tucked behind the garden are the three brightly coloured *roulottes* and the farmhouse, now more or less fully restored. You can choose your *roulotte* according to taste and price: *des amoureux* wears a nostalgic 50s interior; *des manèges* is more reminiscent of the 20s; *des étoiles*, the biggest, is decorated with sequined cushions and natty trinkets from the Orient.

Whichever you choose, you'll have a comfortable night's slumber and the satisfaction of sleeping in a tasteful little space that comes with its own en-suite bathroom – all in a field! Breakfast, normally taken in the farmhouse's fabulously rustic dining area, can also be delivered to your caravan, for a reasonable extra charge.

The surrounding Beaujolais region is awash with vineyards and farms, which of course means an abundance of great cheeses, meats and wines – an excellent reason to get out and sample the wares. Thankfully you can walk or cycle all the overconsumption off easily enough as there are plenty of options to strike out and explore the countryside.

The site lies on the 500-year-old Saint-Jacques de Compostelle pilgrim route, and there are plenty of interesting places to stop in at during your jaunts. Organic wine lovers will enjoy Domaine du Crêt de Ruyère (www.cretderuyere.com). It's a small but perfectly formed vineyard set in the hills above Villié-Morgon and is run by Cathy (English) and Jean-Luc Gauthier.

There are also a few local towns worth exploring. Nearby Avenas has a nice little church (and a great restaurant, see below). Fishing trips can be arranged at attractive Beaujeu (6 miles/10 km), the capital of the Beaujolais (ask at reception). And just 19 miles (30 km) away is Cluny, with its world-famous Benedictine monastery.

And do try to sneak a peek at Pascal's workshop. A carpenter and furniture restorer by trade, he decided to try his hand at making customised *roulottes* and now sells them across France. Far from simply depositing a few caravans in a field, the folk at Les Roulottes de la Serve celebrate the finer aspects of this unique lifestyle and provide an authentically rustic experience.

THE UPSIDE: Unique caravan-in-a-field experience.

THE DOWNSIDE: It's a little hard to find – you need to keep your eyes peeled for the signs – and there's no public transport to the site.

THE DAMAGE: The *roulottes* are individually priced for 2 people per night from €47 (smallest) to €60 (largest).

THE FACILITIES: The *roulottes* have en-suite toilets and showers. Breakfasts are served in the gorgeous farmhouse.

FOOD AND DRINK: The main local restaurant is the Auberge du Fût d'Avenas (69430 Avenas; 00 33 4 74 69 90 76). It's set in an old farmhouse and run by a hip young French couple (Émile and Julien) who speak great English and cook up daily set-menus based on fresh ingredients. Plus, there are markets in Cluny (Saturdays), Villefranche (Mondays) and Belleville (Tuesdays).

FAMILY FUN: For the kids there are lots of safe tree-climbing options and *voie verte* (literally, 'green path') cycling in the area. And the Association de Rollers Clunisois (00 33 3 85 50 29 96) offers lessons for both beginners and experienced roller-skaters.

TREAT YOURSELF: To a hot-air balloon ride across the Beaujolais. Montgolfière Air Escargot is based in Cluny (00 33 3 85 87 12 30).

GETTING THERE: From Lyon take the A6/E15 to Mâcon. Turn off onto the D18 at Belleville. Follow the D18 towards Avenas/Ouroux. The site is signposted from Avenas.

PUBLIC TRANSPORT: Trains and buses serve Belleville. Pick-ups can be organised in advance.

OPEN: Apr–Oct.

IF IT'S FULL: There aren't many other campsites in the region, but there's a wonderful wood-and-stone B&B (Ferme du Planet; 00 33 4 74 04 64 89) just along the road in Ouroux. It's all hand-built (Pascal helped with the wood) and is run by the local vet and his family. Prices for the ridiculously comfortable rooms range from €50 to €60.

Les Roulottes de la Serve, 69860 Ouroux	t	00 33 4 74 04 76 40	w	www.lesroulottes.com

indigo royat

Selecting which campsite to go to requires evaluating the demographic of your travelling party, flicking through each individual's wish list before – and this is usually the interesting part – emptying the piggy bank to assess funds. Beaches, nature, peace and adventure feature in most top five requisites, so why would anyone elect to spend precious holidays next to a city in mainland France? Volcanoes.

But more about them later. First, we'll point out Indigo Royat's own advantages. Right at the foot of the Puy de Dôme on the fringes of the city of Clermont-Ferrand is this fun park ideal for families. Parents with kids over five will fall into the staff's hospitable arms like long-lost lovers, romanced by the site's high hillside location and its effective execution of well-planned facilities.

If you are *sans enfants*, then don't discount this site outright, but do arrive in full anticipation of the daily clamour of children. Since it's geared towards families, the campsite has a swimming pool, a pizza café and hosts morning kids' clubs, as well as sport tournaments and themed evenings with food and dancing. Everyone feels welcome, looked after and safe.

Indigo Royat is one of five Camping Indigo operations in France. Together with the company's three Huttopia campsites they adhere to an environmental policy, which gives them an important edge over rival campsites of this size. Huttopia place great emphasis on eco-tourism, building their gypsy-style caravans and Yukon-style tents to complement nature, whilst at Indigo it's more simplistic: hedgerows are left to grow naturally, the land is nurtured and recycling keenly encouraged.

When you're this close to the Parc Naturel Régional del Volcans d'Auvergne, home to the largest group of volcanoes in Europe, pollution of any kind is a serious *faux pas*. The Auvergne region has over 80 extinct volcanoes, which (you'll be glad to hear) have not erupted for more than 6000 years but have instead turned into prime tourist spots – the hardened magma from the summits has formed around the hilltops creating an unusual sight. There are remarkable vantage points to see the surrounding glaciers and lakes, flora and fauna and it's also a supreme setting in which to try out hand-gliding or hot-air ballooning. Non-thrill-seekers, on the other hand, will enjoy taking photographs from somewhere like Puy de Sancy – the highest mountain in central France – which you can walk up or take the cable car from Mont Dore (18 miles/30 km away from Royat).

Camping Indigo sits atop Royat, an old spa village that boasts the remains of a Roman bath, within the Massif Central – a huge area of mountains and plateaus in south-central France. The beautiful countryside of Auvergne is made up of various *départements* including Puy-de-Dôme and one of its main cities is Clermond-Ferrand. This sprawling urban hub at the foot of Royat is a 'city of art' and ranks amongst the oldest cities of France. You can see it in its entirety from certain hill spots in Royat, but a closer inspection of its old town, Romanesque basilica and its Renaissance façades is essential.

But, not, of course, as essential as a trip to those volcanoes.

THE UPSIDE: A professionally run campsite in the heart of the Massif Central. And we *did* mention those volcanoes, right?

THE DOWNSIDE: It's more suited for families, and in turn less so for couples.

THE DAMAGE: One night in a tent is €5.30–9.80 with additional people at €4.40–5 and children (2–7 years) €2.50–3.20; weekly rates for chalets €385–790 and Indigo tents €190–470.

THE FACILITIES: There are 200 pitches, but only 50 for tent camping. There's a reception, library, bakery, washing machines, swimming pool, tennis court, TV room, grocery shop, kids' playground, camper van service bay, take-away food, baby's bathroom, disabled toilet and five sanitary blocks. It would be quicker to list what there isn't.

FOOD AND DRINK: The panoramic views from the medieval castle courtyard at Le Paradis restaurant in Royat will keep the young ones quiet, as long as they like duck or fish, which feature heavily on the menu (00 33 4 73 35 85 46).

FAMILY FUN: The campsite organises a 2½ mile (4 km) group walk with 'a theme of witches' in search of the spirit of the wizards. This is an imagination-fuelled trip aided by the setting sun throwing shapes all around the site.

TREAT YOURSELF: Clermont-Ferrand gives you every excuse for a night on the tiles. There's a sleek casino (Allée du Pariou, Royat; 00 33 4 73 29 52 52) near the campsite and bars and discos aplenty *en ville.*

GETTING THERE: Eurostar will get you to the city via Paris. Three hours' drive from Paris and one hour from Lyon on the A71 and A72, Royat is 2½ miles (4 km) west of Clermont-Ferrand. Climbing the hilly Royat from Clermont-Ferrand, take rue de la Grotte and turn left onto the D944 at avenue Jean Jaurès towards Route de Gravenoire. Turn right into the campsite at the top of a hill where the road forks.

PUBLIC TRANSPORT: Ryanair hope to reopen their Stansted to Clermont-Ferrand route by April 2008 but if not Air France run regular services out of Heathrow. The airport is located 18 miles (30 km) away in Aulnat. The train station is 3½ miles (5.5 km) from the campsite. There is a bus that runs from Clermont-Ferrand and stops 600 metres from the campsite. There is also a shuttle bus between Royat and the campsite.

OPEN: Apr–mid-Oct.

IF IT'S FULL: On the other side of the city on the River Allier in Vichy is Camping de la Croix St Martin (99 avenue des Graviers, 03200 Abrest; 00 33 4 70 32 67 74; www.camping-vichy.com). This family site has a pool and games room.

Camping Indigo Royat, Route de Gravenoire, 63130 Royat	t	00 33 4 73 35 97 05	w	www.camping-indigo.com

près des étangs

It's a long drive to Cassaniouze, so just take your time to enjoy the wonderful scenery. Seeing the sheer extent of uninhabited land can be overwhelming. There's a serene quality to the way the valleys and hills bump into the horizon, like a collage of rounded building bricks in all shades of green. Passing by your side for miles, undisturbed by roads and traffic, La Châtaigneraie's hilly terrain will eventually descend into the valleys of the beautiful Lot region.

A municipal campsite, Près des Étangs is a simple, modest holiday park. There are six wooden huts, three larger chalets and room for 30 tents. A wonderful natural lake set against a backdrop of verdurous hillocks and trees dominates the space on the site.

Everything around you looks lush and green, even the tents seem to glow with a jade hue.

Early morning, nothing can be heard except perhaps the murmur of a tractor nearby. But by lunchtime every pedalo is out on the lake and all the tables are packed with picnicing holidaymakers. To the left of the lake is a man-made pond, where in the afternoons a lifeguard watches over the swimmers.

From the site's central position in the Cantal *département*, each compass point throws up a variety of lush valleys, panoramic hikes and picturesque villages. Staying local, on the other hand, a morning stroll along Cassaniouze's rolling pastures should set you up for a day of doing very little.

THE UPSIDE: There's a gorgeous natural lake and an artificial 'pool' for swimming in.

THE DOWNSIDE: Those never-ending windy roads might put you off going out even if you want to.

THE DAMAGE: Prices are announced just before the season starts, expect to pay about €7 per person per night to camp and between €210 and €340 per week for a hut or chalet.

THE FACILITIES: Hut hirers and campers share the public facilities; the chalets have their own toilet and shower rooms. The showers are basic. There's a lifeguard throughout July and August. An on-site snack bar sells chips, sandwiches, drinks and ice creams.

FOOD AND DRINK: From the site, it'll take over an hour to reach Salers, but it'll be worth it for a lesson in local cheese production. Guided tasting tours run every day (Apr–Oct) and you can lunch here, too (Les Burons de Salers, Route du Puy Mary, 15140 Salers; 00 33 4 71 40 70 71). Salers' well-renowned beef is usually on the menu throughout July and August.

FAMILY FUN: Have some whacky races in pedalos on the lake. Pedalo hire costs €3 for 30 minutes – exercise and fun combined!

TREAT YOURSELF: To a spot of windsurfing or sailing when the pedalos feel too kiddish. An hour's drive away is the École Française de Voile at Puech des Ouilles beach (open July and August 10am–7pm; 00 33 4 71 46 39 15; out of season by appointment, call 00 33 4 71 48 45 34).

GETTING THERE: From Rodez take the D840 to Decazeville then the D663, then D25 until you see the signpost for 'Camping Cassaniouze du Lac'.

PUBLIC TRANSPORT: Ryanair fly to Rodez, from there you can take the bus as far as Decazeville where you'll need to get a taxi for the last 30-minute leg of the journey (Taxi Diaz will do this for around €30; 00 33 5 65 63 04 04).

OPEN: End-June–Sept.

IF IT'S FULL: Back at the village of Saint-Cirq-Lapopie is Camping La Truffière (00 33 5 65 30 20 22; www.camping-truffiere.com). Not as rough-and-ready as the natural setting of Camping Près des Étangs, it opens from April 1st.

Camping Près des Étangs, 15340 Cassaniouze | t | 00 33 4 71 49 90 03

les chenauds

In the quiet countryside of what the French refer to as 'La France profonde' – the rural depths of the country's centre – is the quiet hamlet of Saint-Junien La Bregère. It's a classic one-street village, so small, in fact, that a short snooze in the passenger seat will be enough for you to miss it altogether.

Just beyond the village, as the road winds up round a series of sharp bends through the trees, is Les Chenauds. It's a small site bordered by the quiet road and a lichen-covered fence that holds back the chaotic forest of ferns, creepers and trees that drops into the valley below. At night, there's such a host of unidentified sounds coming out of the forest, even David Attenborough would be hard pushed to know what on earth is going on.

With limited facilities and attractions, this remote spot in deepest nowhere certainly isn't for everybody – and that's just as well really, as there are only eight pitches. But, we love it for that same reason.

It's a wild hide-out on the very edge of civilisation, and a charming and tranquil place to put your feet up for a few days and listen to the menagerie just beyond the garden fence.

THE UPSIDE: Tranquil spot, hosted by friendly English owners.

THE DOWNSIDE: It's rather in the middle of nowhere. Is that a downside? Hmmm.

THE DAMAGE: €8 per night for 2 adults. Additional adults €2 per night.

THE FACILITIES: There is a fairly basic block with showers and toilets and a separate area for washing. There's a standpipe in the campsite for fresh drinking water (*eau potable*).

FOOD AND DRINK: The site is pretty remote, so self-sufficiency works best. There is a Champion supermarket back up the road in Bourganeuf. If you fancy hanging out in some small town *tabac*, head for Peyrat le Château.

FAMILY FUN: Grab your swimmers and set off to Lac de Vassivière, aptly called the Canada of France. It's one of the largest lakes in France. Built in 1950, it hides its artificiality rather well. It has sandy beaches, plenty of options for boating and fishing, and miles of forest trails for walking and cycling.

TREAT YOURSELF: To some Limoges porcelain. Kaolin, the rare form of white clay used to manufacture porcelain, was discovered in the area in the 18th century. In Limoges, 30 miles (48 km) to the west, there are several boutiques on boulevard Louis-Blanc and a museum in the former archbishop's palace.

GETTING THERE: The site is mid-way between Bourganeuf and Peyrat le Château on the D940. Heading south, pass through the small hamlet of Saint-Junien La Bregère and as the road twists up through the woods, look out for the site entrance on your right.

OPEN: Apr–Oct.

IF IT'S FULL: There's a serviceable campsite back up the road in Bourganeuf. Camping Municipal La Chassagne, 23400 Bourganeuf (00 33 5 55 64 07 61).

Camping Les Chenauds, Route de Peyrat le Château, 23400 Saint-Junien La Bregère

t 00 33 5 55 54 91 87 | w www.leschenauds.com

tipis at folbeix

Can you keep a secret? They say there are two kinds of really great campsites: those you want to tell everyone about and those you want to tell no one about and keep for yourself. Nigel and Sheila Harding's tipis at Folbeix in the enchanted forests of La Creuse definitely belong to the latter category. So, can you keep a secret? OK, then let's begin.

The real attraction of this site is that it's a haven of environmentally conscious living. Nestled in a coppiced wood are six snowy-white tipis, each on a raised platform of pine decking made from Forestry Stewardship Council wood and illuminated at night by candle lanterns and solar-powered lights. And if you're still in the dark about the essence of this place, you can grab one of the wind-up torches available, because as you'll quickly learn, sustainability and self-sufficiency are the watchwords here. It's a philosophy that's particularly apt in La Creuse.

This deep, dark region of France is where they used to speak Occitan, the old Romance language from the time of Dante. It's the language in which travelling troubadours used to sing of their lost loves and favourite taverns. Although it is rarely spoken nowadays, there are vestiges of it in the thick local accent, full of rough, strangled vowels, characteristic of the cross between the languages of 'oc' and 'oil' (that's the language of the Languedoc and of northern France). And if this all sounds like something from *The Lord of the Rings* don't worry. Although it's a rich soup of sounds, it's still recognisably French and you'll soon pick it up. But the fact that the accent is so thick is a sign that this area of France has been pretty much left to its own devices for hundreds of years.

Whilst roads were being built all around it, La Creuse was by-passed by the French and by tourists alike. So, the old Gallo–Roman remains were left untouched, the dialect hardened and the forests grew. And what a playground it has produced. There's horse riding, fishing, cycling and walking in abundance. If you've come by car (and can offset the carbon) then take a drive between Le Bourg d'Hem and Beausoleil in the region known as Le Pays de Trois Lacs (the country of three lakes). The road plunges down through wooded gorges to one of the trio of lakes whose peaceful waters reflect the surrounding forests.

It's ironic that the recent construction of better road links means the area is now opening up as a tourist destination. All the more reason to keep the secret to yourself and get out here whilst it's still off most people's holiday radar. As others inhale the smell of cheap jet fuel and onboard alcopops, you could be breathing in the sweet, musty smells of the forest.

Each of the tipis is set in a different part of the wood and apparently some of the people who come here disappear into the trees at the beginning of the week and aren't seen again until it's time to leave. They sit, they watch and listen to the wildlife snuffling about in the undergrowth and they go and play in the mudbath in the middle of the wood, where deer also come to frolic. However, it's worth wandering back to the Hardings' house every now and again. For a start, you can help yourself to fresh herbs from the garden to pep up what's cooking over your campfire. And, what's more, you won't want to miss out on Sheila's industrious output of jams, chutneys and beverages of varying descriptions (and of varying levels of alcoholic potency!). They're the perfect accompaniment to the lifestyle you'll find in your pearly-white tipi in the luscious, silent forests at Folbeix.

THE UPSIDE: A wonderful, natural site with discreet areas for each of the tipis and an eco-friendly philosophy to match.

THE DOWNSIDE: With only six tipis, it is essential to book.

THE DAMAGE: €350 per week or €170 for a 3-day break for up to 2 adults and 2 children. The tariff includes a continental breakfast, with homemade jams and fresh bread collected from the village each morning.

THE FACILITIES: A new facilities block is being built for 2008, including toilets and showers, a cooking area and day room.

FOOD AND DRINK: The theme is very much one of self-sufficiency and eating locally grown produce. There is a market every Friday just up the road in Châtelus-Malvaleix, which also has a *boulangerie* and *pâtisserie*. But if you pine for a night out, try La Bonne Auberge (see TREAT YOURSELF below).

FAMILY FUN: Play hippos in the mudbath. Just remember to use plenty of the eco-friendly detergent available at the site to wash up afterwards.

TREAT YOURSELF: To a local dinner at La Bonne Auberge (1 rue des Lilas, 23600 Nouzerines; 00 33 5 55 82 01 18). It has a delicious dessert option of local cheese known as Creuseois, made from unpasteurised milk. *Délicieux.*

GETTING THERE: In keeping with the philosophy of minimal environmental impact, the site is not signposted and is easy to miss. Heading east from Guéret on the N145, turn off at the sign for Ajain and head for Ladapeyre. In the village take the D990 towards Châtelus-Malvaleix. Folbeix is a mile (1.5–2 km) or so up the road and is little more than a collection of houses on either side of the road. The site is on your right just as you enter Folbeix. Pull in at the ivy-covered house.

PUBLIC TRANSPORT: There is a train station at Guéret, from where the Hardings can arrange to pick you up for the 15-minute journey to the site.

OPEN: May–Sept.

IF IT'S FULL: There's a fine site owned by English couple Neil and Linda Flinton at Fleurat, midway between Guéret and La Souterraine, called Camping Les Boueix (23320 La Creuse; 00 33 5 55 41 86 81; www.campinglesboueix.com).

Tipi Holidays in France, Folbeix	t	00 33 5 55 80 90 26	w	www.vacanesdetipienfrance.com

guédelon
chantier médiéval
ils bâtissent un château fort
2007
PARC
AVENTURE
DES CHÂTELAINES
www.loisirsenmorvan.com
03 86 31 90 10
Marchés fermiers
en Morvan
de mars à octobre 2007
15 rendez-vous avec
la gastronomie,
les savoir-faire
et l'artisanat
31 mars à Château-Chinon

camping des 2 rives

As its name suggests, Camping des 2 (deux) Rives literally offers double trouble in the babbling brook department, occupying a prime location at the confluence of the meandering Mesvrin and the amiable Arroux rivers. The site itself is a large meadow-like expanse of flat grassland, landscaped with paths and trees to create a neat yet natural environment that's very camper friendly.

Located just outside the tiny village of Étang-sur-Arroux, Camping des 2 Rives has been operated and maintained by friendly Dutch couple Arian Schots and Marja van Duin for about five years. Despite being accessible to camper vans, the 65 pitches create a definite campsite vibe: 80% of guests in the summer are tenters.

The pitches are anywhere from 85 sq. m to a whopping 150 sq. m. Many have shade from the trees and a fair few enjoy prime riverside spots. If you want to be riverside then you'll need to book ahead – those happy to be *sans électricité* can request pitches 17 and 18, which trade convenient ampage for killer views.

The grounds are certainly spacious enough to accommodate everyone without any feeling of being cramped. As well as open pitches and mobile homes there are some interesting funky tipis and pyramid tents, plus some trigano 'tunnel' tents. Large caravans (fully equipped) are available all year for rent, too.

The site has adequate, if slightly shabby, facilities. Throughout July and August, the snack bar opens and there's a daily bakery van delivery for delicious French breads and *croissants*. The snack bar carries a great stock of local wines, too, supplied by two local vineyards (visits available in summer). There's a no-frills communal room offering TV, Internet and table football and even a wi-fi connection for those who can't bear to leave their laptops at home.

The toilet blocks, whilst perfectly clean and useable, are quite old and in need of updating. Being located near reception, they're also a sizeable schlep from the riverside spots – a problem the owners are aware of and hope to fix soon with a new *bloc sanitaire* at the other end of the site.

There are no main meals available on site but a well-stocked supermarket is just a 300-metre walk away. And speaking of nearby, Étang-sur-Arroux is small and sweet – but it might not hold your attention for too long, unless, that is, you like clogs. In which case hop into Musée du Sabot (rue des Résistants; 00 33 3 85 82 24 89), a clog museum offering penetrative insights into this ancestral trade.

Slightly more stimulating in cultural and historic terms are: the nearby fortress settlement of Bibracte, which has a fascinating museum of Celtic civilisation; pretty Vézelay and its 9th-century abbey; the Roman city of Autun – built to eclipse Bibracte (it worked); and, last but not least, the world-famous Benedictine abbey of Cluny. All are within an hour or two's drive from the site.

Wine lovers, too, will adore this region. Not only are there plenty of local vineyards in the immediate vicinity, but 25 miles (40 km) away lies Beaune, which produces some of Burgundy's most excellent wines.

With Parc Régional du Morvan close by, there's no shortage of forest walks and tree-climbing to be had. The roads in the region are especially good for cycling, too, and mountain bikes can be hired from the site. Fishing from the river bank is an obvious and pleasant way of whiling away the hours, as is kayaking along the river. The only question once you've picked up your kayak from reception is – which river to choose!

THE UPSIDE: A great riverside location and one of the few that allows campfires.

THE DOWNSIDE: The sanitary blocks are old and a bit of a walk from the riverside pitches.

THE DAMAGE: A pitch costs €5.50–6.50 per night (depending on the size and season); adults are €2.50–2.80, children €1.20–1.80 (depending on season – but not size).

THE FACILITIES: We've complained already about them being a bit worn, but everything works fine. There's a washing machine, a nice playground and wi-fi reception around the whole site.

FOOD AND DRINK: The local supermarket may be your best friend during a stay here. A pizza van visits on Wednesdays and Saturdays. Guinness lovers will flock to the nearby Irish pub in La Chapelle-sous-Uchon. In summer, Étang-sur-Arroux has a market on Sunday mornings selling regional products, and there's a larger one in Autun on Wednesdays and Saturdays.

FAMILY FUN: The roads in the area are great for cycling, and the rivers perfect for kayaking. Further afield, there's tree climbing in Bibracte (00 33 3 86 61 38 19; www.treeclimbing.fr) and an adventure park in Avallon (00 33 3 86 31 90 10; www.loisirsenmorvan.com).

TREAT YOURSELF: To a night in style at Château de Vault de Lugny (00 33 3 86 34 07 86; www.lugny.fr) a four-star hotel-restaurant surrounded by an authentic 13th-century moat, well known for its great kitchen and splendorous 100-acre garden.

GETTING THERE: From Autun to Étang-sur-Arroux follow the N81, direction Moulins/Luzy. Take the D994 to Étang and follow the *centre ville* signs in the direction of Toulon-sur-Arroux. The site is just outside Étang-sur-Arroux, off the D994.

PUBLIC TRANSPORT: Buses and trains run from Autun to the site daily. The train station in the village has a direct connection to Dijon and Nevers.

OPEN: Apr–Oct.

IF IT'S FULL: The owners have an affiliated campsite, Camping La Boutière (www.la-boutiere.com) in a tiny nearby village. It's small, pretty and very natural, plus it has a yurt. But if you'd prefer a bigger site then head to the *Cool Camping* site at La Forêt du Morvan (see p104).

Camping des 2 Rives, 26–28 Route de Toulon, 71190 Étang-sur-Arroux	t	00 33 3 85 82 39 73	w	www.des2rives.com

2007
EGLISE DE POIL
12 08 07
14 08 07
à bergesserin

la forêt du morvan

The Morvan – slap-bang in the centre of Burgundy – is a vast sylvan paradise that spans well over half a million acres and crosses four different *départements*. Home to frondescent firs and perpendicular pines, silent valleys and proud peaks, gushing waterfalls and enormous lakes, it's the kind of luxuriously natural location that promotes either peaceful meditation or pagan mischief, depending on your spiritual outlook.

Sitting right inside this rural wonderland is La Forêt du Morvan, a family-run campsite on a former farm with 24 acres, nearly eight of which are forest. The campsite originally consisted of six pitches, but the new owners – the Hoekstra family from Holland – managed to expand the number magically to 25, with no loss of space or atmosphere.

The pitches are scattered around a rolling, natural meadow, dotted with trees and hedges, with a good distance between them. When you set up camp on the south-facing hill, you'll see that you get a decent amount of sun as well as the most panoramic views of the national park. And it's good to know that if you arrive tent-less, you can always rent one. There are two types – pyramid and bungalow – that sleep up to five people, with private facilities and a car-parking place.

Even ardent campers can have their own private facilities (for an extra charge), located in one of the barns on the campsite – worktop, sink with hot and cold water, refrigerator and shower.

Kids will love it here. Not only is there a gigantic natural playground a welly throw from the tents, there's also a children's park with a swing, sandpit, trampoline and a see-saw. And if you're unlucky and pitch up on a rainy day, the kids can tussle in the barn (with its own hay attic) or set up a tournament in the covered games space with – amongst other things – ping-pong, table football, table billiards and darts. You won't notice that there's no swimming pool, because taking a dip in either of the two spring-fed swimming lakes is refreshing and fun. And as if that's not enough, the informal on-site kids 'club' arranges sport matches (grown-ups also allowed).

There's not much in the way of food on-site, but the owners have a vegetable patch and enjoy cooking – and are often happy to knock something up for the guests, usually tasty meat, potato and vegetable dishes or the occasional pizza to take back to the tent. And, the barn doubles up as a live music and disco venue, with a karaoke machine and serious speakers to rock the house!

From this perfect base you can literally strike out in any direction or hire mountain bikes and explore this beautiful nature reserve. If you're lucky you may spot any of over 150 species of bird, plus wild boar, deer, badgers and bats.

There are six major lakes, which have an abundance of carp, perch, pike and trout – fishing aficionados will be more than happy. As will water-lovers: the rivers and lakes around offer plenty of watersports. Rivers such as the Chalaux and Cure are great for kayaking and white-water rafting, whilst the lakes offer the opportunity to sail, canoe or just pootle around on a pedalo.

If all the fresh air is making you feel dizzy, then set off to fill up on some culture. The religious sites of Vézelay, and the cultural towns of Avallon and Autun also lie within the Parc Naturel Régional du Morvan. In the village of Château Chinon is the Musée de Septennat (6 rue du Château; 00 33 3 86 85 19 23), which displays the myriad gifts sent to the President of France from all over the world. If that's just not interactive enough for you, in the summer tourists are welcome to join an archaeological dig at Bibracte, a former capital of the Gallic empire, just over 4 miles (7 km) north of the campsite.

With so many interesting possibilities on your doorstep, it might be a struggle to stay still long enough to achieve some of that aforementioned meditation. But with the forest literally all around, you can always get a bit of peace and quiet in before breakfast, before letting your mischievous inner heathen take over.

THE UPSIDE: An *aire naturelle* right in the middle of a nature park.

THE DOWNSIDE: You can't get here using public transport; caravans longer than 6 m may come a cropper on the steep driveway. Is that a downside?

THE DAMAGE: A pitch for a family (5 people) and tent is €15–25 per night, depending on season. A rented tent (sleeps 5) is €47.50–57.50. Private facilities cost €7.50 per night.

THE FACILITIES: In the farm's barns, the toilets and showers are rustic but work fine, and if you'd rather not share you can hire your own toilet/shower combo unit. Kids are well catered for, and there's also a snack bar and a shop selling basics.

FOOD AND DRINK: Morvan is famous for specialties such as honey, cured ham and *fromage blanc*. Restaurant de la Tour is 2½ miles (4 km) from the campsite in Larochemillay (00 33 3 86 84 23 39) and serves lovely regional specialties in a small, intimate setting.

FAMILY FUN: Autun's Base Nautique du Moulin du Vallon (00 33 3 85 86 95 80) provides itineraries for sailing, pedalos, canoes and kayaks. For a gentler trip down the Cure (that's the river, not the band) call AB Loisirs in Saint-Père (00 33 3 86 33 38 38); there is also a zoo in Autun.

TREAT YOURSELF: To a hot-air balloon tour across the countryside (Air Adventures; 00 33 3 80 90 74 23; www.airadventures.fr).

GETTING THERE: From Paris, take the A6 and exit Pouilly-en-Auxois, then the D981/N81 direction Autun–Luzy. From Lyon take the A6 and exit Chalon-sur-Saône sud; then the N80 direction Le Creusot, and N70 direction Montceau-les-Mines, D102 Toulon-sur-Arroux, and D985 to Luzy. From Luzy head to the D27, direction Chateau Chinon/Mont Beuvray. The site is approx 5km after the 2nd turn off to Larochemillay.

OPEN: Apr–Oct.

IF IT'S FULL: Try the *Cool Camping* site of Camping des 2 Rives (see p100). It's also Dutch run and has good access to the southern Morvan.

Camping La Forêt du Morvan, 58370 Larochemillay	t	00 33 3 86 30 47 93	w	www.campinglaforet.nl

300 MÉDAILLES
CLERT
NIORT
ET MÉLANGE

camping de nevers

With a dash of riverside romance and a splash of culture nearby, Camping de Nevers is in prime commercial camping territory. But whilst there is a hint of 'holiday camp' here, the owners thankfully haven't gone the full Disney. (And we should all be pleased it's not called 'Neverland'.) With the Loire at your feet, a majestic 15th-century ducal palace in full view, and everything from cathedrals to ceramic museums just a hop, skip or a pole vault away, this is no Mickey Mouse holiday.

On the lower banks of the Loire – one of the last 'wild' rivers in Europe – the campsite spreads its 73 decent-sized pitches over two levels. The upper section, tidily separated by young hedges and trees, is for caravans and motor homes, whilst the tent pitches occupy the best spot – right down by the river.

First impressions are of a fairly commercial site with ordered rows of statics and caravans dominating the initial entrance views. And the neat, organised reception gives you no idea about the sprawling nature of the riverside pitches below. But, venture down to the lower 'tenters' terrace, where you can pitch wherever you like, and the view suddenly opens out to embrace a pretty, palace-dominated riverside scene.

The facilities, updated in 2005, offer something for everyone – a playground, café/snack bar, Internet, shower cubicles and toilets, washing machine and plenty of hot and cold water. If you don't fancy the short trip across the river for your *petit déjeuner*, then order up a fresh French breakfast (bread, coffee and OJ) for a bargain €3. And, if you need them, there are electricity points and water-taps around the site.

Of course, with the town less than a pole vault away (though, the adjacent bridge is a safer crossing option), there's plenty of bars, restaurants and interesting things to see and do on your doorstep.

Nevers – formerly the significant Roman city Noviodunum – is a handsome Burgundy town well-known for its elegant architecture. Meandering around its winsome network of narrow, winding streets you'll encounter ancient houses from the 14th century and celebrated churches, such as the Romanesque–Gothic Cathedral of Saint Cyr-Sainte Julitte.

Since the Romans left, the town has become better known as the French capital of pottery. Earthenware shops abound and, if you like, you can visit the manufacturers of the renowned *Faïence de Nevers* to see exactly how its made. But history and handicrafts aside, there's a racier side to Nevers: the Formula One Grand Prix. Six miles (10 km) away you'll find the Circuit de Magny-Cours, home of the French Grand Prix. If you're a speed freak, you can try out the Magny-Cours racetrack yourself! But if you prefer to sit back and watch, admire the cars in the Museum Ligier F1 – the only museum in Europe with a collection of Formula One vehicles.

Walkers may rejoice in the fact that the long-distance walking path GR3 passes just by the campsite. But one of the best ways to explore is to rent a *vélo* and start pedalling. Bicycles are available for hire directly from the site, and the nearby *voie verte* (cycling path) offers a superbly scenic 8 mile (14 km) ride. A must-see, and only a short bike ride away (10 miles/
16 km), is the stunning medieval village of Apremont-sur-Allier – one of 'the most beautiful villages of France' and host to an 18th-century botanical garden. *En route*, take a breather (and glug some water) at Le Bec d'Allier for the most glorious sweeping panorama that takes in the confluence of the Loire and Allier rivers.

With all these options right at your feet, the glittering ducal palace that greets you each morning from across the river might well be the last thing you get around to visiting. Truly, you've 'Nevers' had it so good.

THE UPSIDE: Great riverside spot with Nevers a stone's throw (well, a really good throw) away.

THE DOWNSIDE: It's not the quietest of sites since the town centre and a road are close by. Riverside tenters can be exposed to the wind.

THE DAMAGE: Two people with a tent and a vehicle costs €12–13. An extra person is €2–3.

THE FACILITIES: All the usuals of showers, toilets (including for disabled access) and laundry are there. You can breakfast on the site and there's a snack bar, and Internet access. Along with the kids' playground, there's *boules* and bicycle hire.

FOOD AND DRINK: Place Carnot in the centre of town is home to several bars and brasseries with terraces. We'd recommend La Mange'oir (00 33 3 86 57 28 61; www.lamangeoir.fr.st), a charming *crêperie* that also serves specialties from the Savoie region. For regional wines try Inter Caves (3 rue Claude Tillier; 00 33 3 86 59 02 37; www.intercaves.fr). There is a market each Saturday in the centre of Nevers.

FAMILY FUN: With the river at your feet, it might be a good idea to teach the kids a spot of fishing. For a faster pace, there's karting at Magny-Cours or a kayak/canoe trip down the Loire.

TREAT YOURSELF: To a day's driving on the Grand Prix track (Magny-Cours; 00 33 3 86 21 80 00; www.magnyf1.com). Driving courses are available all year round.

GETTING THERE: From Paris take the A6 direction Lyon, then A77 Nevers. Take Exit 37 and then head towards Nevers. The campsite is on the right before the bridge. From the south, you also need to get onto the A77 and take the same exit (37).

PUBLIC TRANSPORT: Nevers is served by train and bus. Several connections a day run between Nevers, Paris, Lyon and Dijon. The campsite is a 10-minute walk from the train and bus stations.

OPEN: Mid-Apr–mid-Oct.

IF IT'S FULL: La Saulaie (Quai de la Saulaie; 00 33 3 86 70 00 83) in pretty La Charité-Sur-Loire (18 miles/30 km away) sits on an island between two bridges with views of the historical centre.

Camping de Nevers, rue de la Jonction, 58000 Nevers	t	00 33 6 84 98 69 79	w	www.campingnevers.com

hortus, le jardin de sully

In former times Sully was one of the main strategic crossing points of the Loire and so the extravagant *château* (seat of Maurice de Sully, the Bishop of Paris who commissioned the building of Notre Dame) was more than just ornamental.

Built in the mid-14th century, it was an unwelcome home for Joan of Arc who was held captive here in 1430 by Georges de la Trémoïlle. But it has its lighter side, too. A special theatre was built in the *château* in the 18th century to stage the plays of Voltaire who was a frequent guest to keep the duke amused.

Hortus is on the northern bank of the Loire opposite the town and half a mile or so downstream from the *château*. The camping area itself is adjacent to the pebbly shores of the water. Swing through the gate in the fence and take a leisurely riverside walk back to the bridge and, hey presto, you've arrived in town.

The pitches have handy picnic tables on which to eat your feast of freshly cooked local pork *saucisse* (sausage) with a few shallots. And, this being the Loire, you don't need to look very far to find a nice bottle of plonk with which to wash it all down.

THE UPSIDE: Town views from this compact riverside site, close to the historic *château* of Sully.

THE DOWNSIDE: You can't see the *château* from the site and, compared with some of the other towns on the Loire, Sully does lack a little charm.

THE DAMAGE: Tent, caravan or camper plus 2 adults is €12.50 per night (€15.50 in July and August). Electricity is €4. Additional adults are €3.65 (€5.20) and kids (6–12 years) are €2.10 (€3.15). For just over €35 you can hire one of the bungalow *toiles* – square tents in an area of their own that looks a bit like Genghis Khan's field HQ.

THE FACILITIES: Well-tended though not plentiful. There are toilets and a hot shower in a male and female block, along with a row of dinky outside showers and basins plus a dish-washing area.

FOOD AND DRINK: There's a lively pub called the Castle Tavern (00 33 2 38 36 21 40) on the corner of rue du Grand Sully, just opposite the *château*. For a more intimate feel, take the same road and further up you'll find Le Relax: it's where you'll meet the locals. Between them is one of the better restaurants in town, Côtés et Jardin (00 33 2 38 36 35 89; www.cotes-jardins.fr) in an old limestone-fronted building with a fine dining room.

FAMILY FUN: There is a small play area and two funky inflatable swimming pools that should keep the children occupied for a while.

TREAT YOURSELF: To some *faïence* (fine tin-glazed pottery) from the nearby town of Gien, with its characteristic yellow and blue glaze – much imitated but never bettered.

GETTING THERE: It couldn't be easier. Take the D960 east from Orléans, along the north bank of the Loire. Half a mile before Saint-Père sur Loire, the campsite is on your right, between the road and the river.

PUBLIC TRANSPORT: There is an infrequent bus service between Orléans and Saint-Père sur Loire. On weekdays buses leave Orléans and reach Saint-Père just over an hour later.

OPEN: All year.

IF IT'S FULL: There is a small hostelry on the corner of the bridge on the north bank of the Loire just as you enter Saint-Père sur Loire (Hostellerie du Château, 4 Route du Paris; 00 33 2 38 36 24 44; www.hostellerie-du-chateau.fr).

Hortus, Le Jardin de Sully, Route d'Orléans 45600 Saint-Père sur Loire

t 00 33 2 38 36 35 94 w www.camping-hortus.com

les roulottes

The Loire valley, one of France's principal tourist destinations, is disappointingly littered with gargantuan caravan parks displaying stickers of affiliation from just about every caravan club in the EU. So, you'll thank your lucky stars when you find Sené Arnaud, just outside the little town of Huisseau-sur-Cosson, near Blois.

Les Roulottes is a collection of old-fashioned gypsy caravans in a quiet backwater of the countryside that's deliberately difficult to find. Sené, the quietly spoken but very welcoming proprietor of the site, doesn't advertise or put up signs. That just encourages the idly curious and passers-by, he says. No, like some kind of Harry Potter test, first you have to find the place and only then do you deserve to come here. Why? Because Sené takes his three caravans seriously and they are all the genuine article.

There's a 1970 three-person caravan in peaceful shades of mauve and olive, with a raised double bed and a comfortable single like a *chaise longue*. In the middle is a 1950s model that serves as the kitchen/diner and which also houses the compact and tidy bathroom. Finally, there's a stately 1930s double in bright reds and greens with an elegant raised double bed set into rich woodwork. And, as if that weren't heritage enough for you, Sené is in the process of restoring a magnificent wooden-wheeled 1890 caravan to provide yet more accommodation.

Nuzzling up to the banks of a river so slow it looks like a long pond, the site nestles into a small sunken clearing below the road and the bridge, surrounded by trees. It's as private as you could wish for and as quiet as a Marcel Marceau sketch. The caravans are arranged facing a strip of grass with the charcoal ring of an open cooking fire. At night you can sit here whilst cooking up a feast and imagining the strains of a gypsy violin as the sun goes down and the silence deepens around you. And if it's your turn to cook (again), keep the folks amused by telling them the story of Denis Papin, who was born in nearby Chitenay in the 17th century and invented the pressure cooker.

In the morning, after the first night of unbroken sleep you've probably enjoyed in ages, you may just want to lounge by the river watching a fishing rod occasionally twitch. Or chill in the hammock that's strung between the trees, stick a piece of grass in your mouth and pull your hat down

over your eyes (and who's to say you haven't earned it?). But, don't linger long as there's plenty to be getting on with. This is, after all, the Loire valley and you're only a short drive from Blois, one of the finest towns the length of the river.

Before entering Blois, stop on the southern bank and take in the view of the *château*. For architectural buffs, there's plenty to wet the palate, with everything from Gothic to Renaissance to classical revival on show. Once in the town, try not to lose yourself in the huddled streets of the old quarter and find your way to the Tour Beauvoir, which dates all the way back to the 11th century. It's where it all started and the ideal place to learn that the ensuing 900 years of history in Blois are more full of mystery, intrigue, murder and treason than a Christmas weekend playing Cluedo with the in-laws.

A colourful past indeed, but not a patch on the brightly painted four-wheeled cabins back at base.

THE UPSIDE: A simple, unaffected and genuine taste of the gypsy lifestyle.

THE DOWNSIDE: You need to bring your own bed linen; and with only a handful of *roulottes*, it's essential to call ahead.

THE DAMAGE: €450 per week in July and August reducing to €310 the rest of the year. For a 5-night stay, rates are €380/€250; and weekend (Sat–Mon) rates are €200/€150.

THE FACILITIES: Limited to a small toilet and shower in one of the *roulottes*, though they are clean and functional. There are bikes and canoes to use whilst you're at the site.

FOOD AND DRINK: Bring your own to cook on the open fire. There is a hob and microwave in one of the *roulottes* but you'd be a fool not to use the real thing. Otherwise head into Blois, where the locals' favourite restaurant is Au Bouchon Lyonnais (25 rue des Violettes, Blois; 00 33 2 54 74 12 87), serving a mix of local cuisine and, as the name implies, dishes from the most gourmet of French cities, Lyon, in a charming dining room of old wood beams and stone walls.

FAMILY FUN: Take the kids to circus school: L'École de Cirque Micheletty (00 33 2 38 55 13 98; www.ecoledecirquemicheletty.com) at nearby Saint-Jean de Braye has juggling, acrobatics and lessons in the art of clownship.

TREAT YOURSELF: To a day out at Chambord, visiting the magnificent *château* (the most visited in the region) and its extensive woods. It's only a short drive away but worth a full day. If you can, stay until sundown, when a series of coloured floodlights illuminates the *château*.

GETTING THERE: From Blois, follow the D33 towards Huisseau-sur-Cosson. As you approach the town, you will see Château des Grotteaux. Turn left and carry on past the entrance, following the road round behind the *château*. Where the tarmac runs out, take the dirt track to the left, through a small tunnel, and the gated entrance to Les Roulottes is immediately on your left.

OPEN: Late-Mar–Christmas.

IF IT'S FULL: There's a pleasant campsite in Huisseau-sur-Cosson itself (just past the cemetery!) – Camping de Chatillon (6 rue de Chatillon, 41350 Huisseau-sur-Cosson; 00 33 2 54 20 35 26).

Les Roulottes, Les Marais, 41350 Huisseau-sur-Cosson	t	00 33 6 67 74 94 93	w	www.lesroulottes.net

le moulin fort

Walk through the woods along the south bank of the River Cher from the campsite at Le Moulin Fort at dawn. If the weather's good there's every chance you'll start hearing voices from the sky. The gods calling to you at last? Well, you never know. But more likely, it's the occupants of a couple of Montgolfière balloons drifting overhead towards the *château* at Chenonceaux. Keep walking through the trees for five minutes and you'll see why. Built across the river is one of the Loire valley's finest sights. When it catches the morning rays, the sandstone of Chenonceau glows gold and is perfectly reflected in the almost still waters of the river. It probably looks even better from the basket of a balloon but if you don't have a head for heights, you can always catch the *bateau mouche* that operates from the riverbank opposite the campsite.

The charmingly appointed site of Le Moulin Fort occupies a strip of river bank along the Cher river, one of the tributaries of the Loire. Just a little upriver from the *château* and a stone's throw from a weir, it's overlooked by willows, fringed by waist-high grass and is a perfect picture of sleepy French tranquillity. It's the kind of place that makes you realise that weeping willows and lazy water somehow go together like baguette and cheese, onions and berets, Gainsbourg and Birkin. Le Moulin Fort has the kind of lackadaisical air that will have you sitting staring into space whilst time ticks by almost as slowly as the waters of the river. Before you know it, the sun will be going down, the waters darkening, and you'll wonder where on earth the day went.

But before you idle away your entire life on the river bank, remember that this is the Loire and there's a lot to see. And where better to start than Chenonceaux? The town, unlike the *château*, is spelt with an 'x' for some strange reason best known to the scholars of the Académie Française, who zealously oversee the French language and object to words like '*le weekend*' and '*le pique-nique*' creeping like a canker into their vocabulary.

Chenonceaux is a picture-postcard kind of place with ivy-clad hostelries and narrow streets of honey-coloured buildings, vaguely reminiscent of the Cotswolds. The *château* itself is open daily and costs €9.50 to enter but it is worth it just for the gardens and the views alone. Catherine de Medici laid out some of the parks and added one of the galleries around the time when Mary Queen of Scots was a visitor.

The nearby town of Amboise has another of the most picturesque *châteaux* of the Loire, sitting high on its ramparts on the south bank of the river. The town is also famous for being the last residence of one of the world's great artists, Leonardo da Vinci. Da Vinci spent his final years at Le Clos Lucé in Amboise on a pension of 1000 *écus soleils* (that's quite a lot), all courtesy of François I who was a fan of Leonardo's work. Not such a man of taste, though, to spot his most famous painting. It is rumoured that the Mona Lisa, never much of a hit during the artist's lifetime, used to sit in a corner of his studio, leaning against the wall. Perhaps that's why she looks so rueful – though, sometimes you wonder if she wouldn't rather swap her current abode on the wall behind bullet-proof glass at the Louvre in Paris for the quieter surroundings of Leonardo's house at Amboise. Or even a spot overlooking the willow trees at Le Moulin Fort.

THE UPSIDE: Idyllic site on the willowy banks of a quiet tributary of the Loire, spoiled only by…

THE DOWNSIDE: …the new extension to the A85 motorway has recently opened to the south of the site and there is a railway line on the opposite bank with occasional passing trains.

THE DAMAGE: Tent, caravan or camper van plus 2 adults is between €13.50 and €22 depending on the season. Additional adults are between €3 and €5 and children (4–12) are charged at €2–4. Electricity is €4.

THE FACILITIES: Two good clean *blocs sanitaires* with separate male and female facilities, including hot (well, warm) showers. There is a busy bar/restaurant in the mill house (often so busy you'll need to book) that serves decent but not spectacular grub and beer. There's also a swimming pool, kid's pool and a small play area.

FOOD AND DRINK: The best meals are to be had across the river on the terrace of La Roseraie (7 rue du Docteur Bretonneau, Chenonceaux; 00 33 2 47 23 90 09). Also in the village the Cave des Dômes (00 33 2 47 23 90 07) sells the wine that's bottled at the *château*.

FAMILY FUN: There are bikes for hire at the campsite for you to enjoy the quiet back roads of the Cher.

TREAT YOURSELF: To a hot-air balloon flight over the *château* (about €160 per person, including children – who must be of a certain age or height to be able to see over the edge of the basket). The dawn flights afford unrivalled views of the Loire valley and Château de Chenonceau in the middle of the River Cher.

GETTING THERE: Follow the D976 east from Tours on the south bank of the Cher, bypassing Bléré. There's a main junction between the villages of Francueil and Chenonceaux. Turn left there, heading for Chenonceaux, and the campsite is along the banks of the river, just before the bridge on your right.

OPEN: Apr–Sept.

IF IT'S FULL: The nearest decent site is the municipal site at Chenonceaux (00 33 2 47 23 90 13) across the river.

Camping Le Moulin Fort, 37150 Francueil-Chenonceaux	t	00 33 2 47 23 86 22	w	www.lemoulinfort.com

Blacks

la vendette

Part of the Huttopia chain's Indigo brand of sites, Camping La Vendette is as good as it gets for beachside camping. Given that it is only a little south of Brittany, just below the mouth of the Loire, Noirmoutier is like a slice of the Mediterranean. It's no surprise that Renoir came here in the 1890s to paint the shimmering greens and purples of the pine shade. From the whitewashed villas with terracotta roof tiles and blue wooden shutters to the cool blue waters and abundant woods, this place seems to be a couple of hundred miles north of where it should be. When the weather's right, you can lie back and watch the children paddle in the still waters while out in the sheltered bay little boats bob at anchor. And you'll ask yourself 'who needs the Med?' It all just seems a bit too good to be true.

Admittedly the site is a bit of a hike out of town by the main roads but there's a handy short cut through a nature reserve along a road that's closed to traffic. The town itself has sleepy streets of sun-bleached houses, a medieval castle and a Romanesque church, which was formerly part of a Benedictine abbey. Sure, the place has its share of tourists and postcard shops but it retains a certain cutesy charm.

Back in Renoir's day, Île de Noirmoutier was accessible only by boat or by a cobbled causeway called the Passage du Gois that was submerged at high tide. Nowadays there's a bridge connecting the southern tip of the island to the mainland, though it makes for a longer round-trip than cutting across from Beauvoir-sur-Mer. Besides, if you get your timing and the tide right, it's still more fun to drive across the causeway. Luckily the island's remoteness and the difficulty of access means that the tourists don't arrive in droves.

In town there's a fine terrace café from under whose yellow awning you can watch the world go by while you sip a *petite noisette* and chew ruminatively on a *pain au chocolat*. Fortified and refreshed you can stroll out to the open-air saltpans, which form the backbone of the local economy. Like far eastern paddy fields missing the green shoots of rice, the marshes have been dug into square channels in which seawater is trapped and allowed to evaporate under the scorching sun. You can buy the *fleurs de sel* in town, along with the local fishermen's latest catch and then head back to the site to cook up a really tangy treat.

Choose a beachside pitch or retreat deeper into the shady pines – there are no manicured lawns with hissing sprinklers on this site. Just kick a few pine cones out of the way and pitch your tent between the trees (*Pinus pinaster* if you're at all arboreally inclined – they were planted in the 19th century apparently to help anchor the sand, which admittedly is a little shifty). The whole area, known as the Bois de la Chaize, is a magical tangle of trees alive with birdlife. After your seafood supper, if you turn left out of the site and follow the road through the wood of pine, ilex and mimosa, you'll emerge from the trees between a flat water meadow and a sheltered bay, and you might just be treated to a fantastic view of the silhouette of castle, church and town against the setting sun. Perfect.

THE UPSIDE: Fantastic pine-shaded site right on a quiet beach. You just can't get a better-located seaside site than this.

THE DOWNSIDE: In July and August there's a €3.50 supplement for a beachside pitch – which is a bit cheeky.

THE DAMAGE: A pitch is €12.90 (€18.10 in high season) plus €3.20 per adult (€4.40) and €1.50 (€2.30) for children (2–7 years). Electricity is between €3.20 and €5.

THE FACILITIES: Not quite up to the standard of the Huttopia site at Versailles (p48) but pretty good. Plenty of hot showers, toilets and other washing facilities. The washing machines and driers take tokens (*jetons*), from reception.

FOOD AND DRINK: There's a *boulanger* who comes to the site every morning with fresh bread and other goodies. Catch him outside reception at 8.30am. For a great dining experience, go to Le Grand Four on the corner above the castle (00 33 2 51 39 61 97; www.legrandfour.com). It's a beautiful ivy-clad building, with a couple of tables outside fabulously lorded over by the huge castle walls. Set menus start at €18.

FAMILY FUN: Time your arrival or departure with the low tide and take the famous Passage du Gois to or from the *île*. Be warned, though, that you don't want to dawdle or the rising tide will get, you…just like in *Chitty Chitty Bang Bang*.

TREAT YOURSELF: To some salt. That's right – there is a thriving salt industry on the island and there's a marvellous little shop opposite the castle on rue de Grand Four called Château de Sel.

GETTING THERE: The sites (there are several along Les Sableaux) are well signposted from the main road through the town. La Vendette is the last of them on the left with a large blue banner over the entrance.

OPEN: Late-Apr–Sept.

IF IT'S FULL: Right next door (but without the same access to the beach) is the municipal site of Le Clair Matin (00 33 2 51 39 05 56). It's a perfectly nice site with a few shady pitches and some around a cleared lawn next to the road.

Camping La Vendette, 23 allée des Sableaux, Bois de la Chaize, 85330 Noirmoutier-en-L'île

t 00 33 2 51 39 06 24 w www.camping-indigo.com

les sables d'argent

This rugged place is the way seaside sites are meant to be. You can tell it's windy by the shape of the trees, which look like people trying to hang on to inside-out umbrellas. With nothing to hold back the full force of the Atlantic, no sandbars to cushion the blow of the waves or quiet paddling lagoons here, the site is pretty exposed, particularly if you pitch right on the dune where the full force of the gale sweeps in from the sea. But, then, the crash of the breakers and the sound of canvas straining against the guy ropes is what it's all about.

From the pitches right on the dune, you can look down on this great expanse of sand and the grey-blue Atlantic stretching to the skyline, feel the wind in your hair and taste the salt on your tongue, and realise you're looking straight out onto Poseidon's playground.

You may also end up pondering our fascination for extremities, why we're drawn to the furthest point and land's end. Well, part of the answer is places like this. When you climb to the top of the dune next to the campsite, all you have before you is sand, sea and sky. It's so uncluttered, so simple, that it acts like a course of cranial irrigation but without the need to stick a hosepipe in your ear.

Situated near the northern tip of Pointe de Médoc, the spit of land between the Atlantic and the estuary of the Gironde, the town of Soulac-sur-Mer is one of those weird, unsettling places that you know is only really alive for six months of the year. It hibernates in the winter when the tourists have gone and the red-brick buildings are shuttered and empty. Mind you, the town can't go completely to sleep – apparently the sands have a habit of trying to bury it. The church was once overwhelmed by a dune and had to be dug out by the townsfolk. Perhaps that's why there are so many bucket-and-spade shops in town.

Of course, the Médoc is famous for more than church-swallowing sand dunes. Up the eastern side of this long finger of land lie some of the best-known vineyards in France. If your cellar has bottles from half the *châteaux* up here, you're probably running an expensive restaurant in Mayfair. Margaux, Moulis, Pomerol, Pauillac and Saint-Julien are just a few of the prestigious wines from these parts. Woe betide anyone who ends up as designated driver when you're cruising around the region, stopping off for a few *dégustation* sessions as you go. And cursed be the car boot so full of camping gear that there's no room for a case or two of wine, bought direct from the *château*.

Up the other side of the Gironde is the Côte d'Argent – miles and miles of silver sand, towering pines and flat marshland dotted with inland lakes. The bare soil is a real contrast to the fertility of the vineyards just a few miles to the east but it is this ruggedness that gives the area its curious allure. So, if you've come up through the vineyards, head back down this side of the Gironde, past the huge Lac d'Hourtin-Carcans, a place of marshes, dunes and forests, and stop off at the resort of Lacanau-Océan to watch the surfers riding the huge breakers that batter the beach. This stretch of sand reaches all the way down to the Arcachon basin and the clean air will help dispel any grogginess that may linger after your visit to the vineyards.

THE UPSIDE: Magnificently rugged, sandy, wind-in-the-hair camping.

THE DOWNSIDE: A few too many statics and next door is the ugly municipal sports stadium.

THE DAMAGE: Tent or caravan/campervan plus 2 adults is €15.95 (€19.95 in July and August). Additional adults are €3/€4.50 and children (2–10) are €2.70/€3.50. Electricity is €3.90.

THE FACILITIES: Decent amenities block with hot showers, though not too many toilets. Dishes and clothes washing facilities are also available.

FOOD AND DRINK: There's a small bar on the site but head to The Neptune (12 rue de la Plage; 00 33 5 56 73 32 50) that has a lively terraced bar serving – you guessed it – fresh seafood.

FAMILY FUN: Bikes can be hired from the site for €12 a day. There is a comprehensive network of cycle paths all up and down the coast. They're perfectly safe for families as they wend their way through the forests well away from the roads.

TREAT YOURSELF: To a visit to one of the *châteaux* and its vineyard. Be warned, though, that the most famous ones – such as Château Lafite Rothschild (00 33 5 56 73 18 18; www.lafite.com) and Château Margaux (00 33 5 57 88 83 83; www.chateau-margaux.com) – get booked up weeks in advance, so plan ahead.

GETTING THERE: A long drag up the D1/N215 from Bordeaux (it's over 50 miles/80 km). Follow the signs into town on the D1 and take a left onto boulevard de l'Amélie. The site is on the right, just past the municipal sports stadium.

PUBLIC TRANSPORT: Trains run from Bordeaux to Soulac-sur-Mer. The station is about half a mile (0.8 km) from the campsite.

OPEN: Easter–Sept.

IF IT'S FULL: There are plenty of sites in town but for something different carry on down the coast for half a mile (0.8 km) to L'Amélie where there's Camping L'Amélie Plage (33780 Soulac-sur-Mer; 00 33 5 56 09 87 27; www.camping-amelie-plage.com) overlooking La Pointe de la Négade.

Les Sables d'Argent, 33 boulevard de l'Amélie, 33780 Soulac-sur-Mer

t 00 33 5 56 09 82 87 w www.sables-d-argent.com

panorama du pyla

The great sand dune at Pyla is nearly 120 metres high, 450 metres wide and extends for a mile and a half down the Atlantic coast south of Arcachon. That's a whole heap of sand and would make a fantastic castle for sure, but you'd need a JCB rather than a bucket and spade. Luckily, easier options are on offer. You can climb it, sit at the bottom and dangle your feet in the sea or just roll back your tent flaps, lie back and admire it, because this campsite is right on the southern end of the dune.

Part of the Yelloh! group that runs nearly 40 sites around France, Panorama du Pyla is fairly large and commercial, and it's pricier than average. But what you get for your euros is the location. The site is superbly set on sloping, sandy, pine-shaded terraces abutting a cliff overlooking the sea. Out in the waters is a nature reserve, the Banc d'Arguin, whose constantly shifting sandbars are revealed at low tide.

Looking north, the views up the coast extend past the entrance to the Bassin d'Arcachon up to the lighthouse on the point at Cap Ferret. Behind the site is a vast expanse of ancient forest stretching over the hills to the horizon.

And just a short drive north is the town of Arcachon, a once fashionable 19th century winter resort for the rich and famous, built when the railway line was extended from Bordeaux to the coast. Owners of the great *châteaux* of the Bordeaux wine-making region kept holiday homes here and more recently it attracted the likes of Marilyn Monroe.

The town may have lost a little of its cachet but it is still an interesting place and offers fantastic views over the Bassin d'Arcachon. Here oyster farms litter the lagoon around the Île aux Oiseaux and herons, storks and the occasional migrating greylag goose can be spotted stalking the fish reservoirs at the eastern shore of the bay. You can even catch your own dinner thanks to the abundance of seafood revealed at low tide. In addition to easily gathered goodies such as mussels, clams and razor-clams, a little more ingenuity (and a net) could have you dining on tasty shrimp or crab.

Back at base you'll be able to watch the sea bash the sandbar as your *fruits de mer* sizzle in the pot. If you look up through the pine trees that cover this site, you'll see squadrons of paragliders riding the

GRADIENT

thermals that rise up from the shore along the cliff. They're often so close as they glide past the site, you feel you ought to reach out, shake hands and introduce yourself. But if you choose not to, the only sound you'll hear is the slight whisper of wind over parachute silk as they pass by on their way to landing on the dunes like colourful butterflies. Forget whale song or tantric chanting; the soporific flutter and flap of the circling gliders is just as peaceful and relaxing as any ambient CD.

Occasionally the peace is broken as a phalanx of thundering choppers sweeps the bay. Don't be alarmed by this *Apocalypse Now* moment, they're just visiting from the military base next door – probably on a reconnaissance mission for the next platoon camping holiday amongst the shady conifers. After all, who doesn't love the smell of fresh pine needles in the morning?

THE UPSIDE: Spectacular pitches on a cliff-top next to the largest sand dune in Europe.

THE DOWNSIDE: It's quite pricey.

THE DAMAGE: A pitch plus 2 adults (including electricity) ranges from €17 to €40 per night, depending on the season. Additional adults are €4–7 and under-12s are €3–4.

THE FACILITIES: Plentiful, clean blocks with sea-breeze ventilation but the supply of hot water for the showers can be patchy.

FOOD AND DRINK: There is a small shop on site for basic provisions and a rather fine restaurant in the middle of the site called Le Panorama that overlooks the sea and serves such goodies as great slabs of duck with red fruit and goat's cheese in a crispy *crêpe*. There's a fairly fancy wine list, too.

FAMILY FUN: There are two swimming pools with a water slide that's a big hit with the kids.

TREAT YOURSELF: To some paragliding. Novices can enjoy tandem flights with an instructor or, if you're qualified, you can fly solo. The company – École Winover (Aérodrome, 40600 Biscarrosse; 00 33 6 14 15 32 73) – operates from the campsite and also runs microlight flights from the nearby airfield.

GETTING THERE: From Bordeaux, follow the A63/A660 towards Arcachon. Come off at La Teste de Buch and follow the signs for Dune du Pyla. There's a single road running between the forest and the dune, and Camping Panorama du Pyla is the third site on the right.

OPEN: Apr–Sept.

IF IT'S FULL: There are five sites along the dune: Pyla Camping (00 33 5 56 22 74 56) is right next door to Camping Panorama du Pyla and has access to the beach. Back up the road, both Camping de la Dune (00 33 5 56 22 72 17) and Camping La Forêt (00 33 5 56 22 70 50) sit at the bottom of the dune.

Camping Panorama du Pyla, Grande Dune du Pyla, Route de Biscarrosse, 33315 Pyla-sur-Mer

	t	00 33 5 56 22 10 44	w	www.camping-panorama.com

SALEWA

cap de l'homy

Municipal sites in France can be a bit hit and miss, even with the star-rating system, but this one is worth all the stars in a modest-sized galaxy. There's something about a campsite with pine trees, sand and the sound of waves breaking on a beach; Cap de l'Homy makes good use of this formula. A touch on the large side for some tastes, its advantage is that there's plenty of room to kick back and spread out, whether you want to be near the dunes or buried deep in the trees, which extend well back from the sands into La Forêt de Lit-et-Mixe.

Most visitors to Cap de l'Homy, however, come for the sea. The site has what is virtually a private beach miles from anywhere else. Situated on the incredible stretch of silver-sanded coastline running all the way from Soulac-sur-Mer to Biarritz, this place has formed a curious little township for itself. It's a short walk up over the sands to the beach or you can take a detour into the collection of shops that has sprung up as an amenities centre for the campsite. The reason it's so remote is that the coastal road running down the western side of the Gironde is about 4 miles (6.5 km) inland. Every few miles there's a road heading for the coast but there's no direct connection between the coastal townships. So, the beach for a few miles north and south of each settlement is fairly inaccessible and usually deserted.

Like the larger town of Lacanau-Océan to the north and the increasing popular Biarritz to the south, Cap de l'Homy is popular with surfers. The waves roll in uncontested onto the beach and conditions can occasionally be challenging, though it's not really for hardcore ripcurlers. If you are a more experienced surfer, you're better off heading down to Biarritz, where the rocks and the currents make for a more testing (and upmarket) setting. Cap de l'Homy, on the other hand, is an ideal spot for beginners to learn the tricks of the waves, partly because there aren't too many people around to laugh at you and partly because the local surfing school offers a guarantee that beginners will be standing up by the end of their first lesson.

And if surfing leaves you bored, head back up the forest road to explore the nearby villages of Lit-et-Mixe, Saint-Julien-en-Born and Mézos, none of which is very big but each has a weekly market selling local produce. Further to the north is the resurrected town of Mimizan, which has twice been buried by the inexorable advance of the sands – the first time was as far back as the 6th century. It's also worth exploring the waterways of the Courat de Contis and the peaceful inland lakes, particularly the Étang de Léon, which offers a variety of watersports to the non-surfer.

And after all that activity, take a trip to Dax, which is the Bath of France – dating back to Roman times and famous ever since for its hot springs, hot mud and spas. But if all that sounds like too much effort for you, just sit back in the shade of the pines, put your feet up and do nothing more strenuous than stretching out to pluck another beer from the cool box.

THE UPSIDE: A remote stretch of virtually private silver-sanded beach.

THE DOWNSIDE: There's not much here apart from the beach.

THE DAMAGE: A pitch plus a vehicle and 2 adults is between €11.20 and €16.30 depending on the season. A camper van plus 2 adults is between €8.10 and €13. Additional adults are €3.50–5 and children under 13 €2–3. A *bungalow toile* is €200–500 per week.

THE FACILITIES: Good, clean and plentiful, as you'd expect from a French municipal site.

FOOD AND DRINK: For basic provisions, there is a modest shopping area in Cap de l'Homy with a *pâtisserie*, a small supermarket and a newsagent. For a wider selection, head to Lit-et-Mixe, which also has a market selling local produce, including *pastis*.

FAMILY FUN: As well as the beach, of course, there is a games hut for kids, along with a small play area within the site itself.

TREAT YOURSELF: To some surfing lessons from Cap Surf Cool (00 33 6 86 21 54 32; www.capsurfcool.com). They operate from a hut just to the left of the car park at the top of the sand dune; open from June to September.

GETTING THERE: From Bordeaux follow the A63 (E5/E70) *autoroute* south towards Bayonne. Come off at junction 14 on the D38 heading for Mézos and Saint-Julien-en-Born. From the latter town, follow the D652 through Lit-et-Mixe and a mile or so out of town turn right on the D88 and follow the road through the forest all the way to Cap de l'Homy. The campsite is the first thing you'll come to on the right.

OPEN: May–Sept.

IF IT'S FULL: The remote nature of the coastline here makes this an isolated spot – which is probably why there's a naturist site further south at Arnaoutchot (00 33 5 58 49 11 11) run by France4naturisme. If you can bare it.

Camping Municipal du Cap de l'Homy, 600 avenue de l'Océan, 40170 Lit-et-Mixe

t 00 33 5 58 42 83 47 w www.camping-cap.com

Quechua

domaine le poteau

Budding wine buffs who've thought about signing up for a wine tasting trip in an authentic vineyard, but haven't got round to it, read on. In the heart of Gers' bountiful wine- and Armagnac-producing *département* is a Dutch-run campsite where they grow enough grapes in their own backyard to make 20,000 bottles of wine a year.

You get a real taste for agricultural France as you pass tractors chugging along roads lined with tall trees that have grown from either side of the road and have entwined together above you. There are as many of these tree tunnels as there are vineyards around Castelnau d'Auzan, the nearest village to the campsite, a scene that's as refreshing to the eyes as putting cucumber slices on them.

If you can avoid wheel spinning on the gravel drive, park up, go walk about and you'll soon spot the rigid vines shooting up behind the owners' house. It's a look that complements their sprawling garden. There's an assortment of shrubbery, small trees and bushes to obscure your tent from your neighbours, whilst across the driveway, a covered dining area and a cute terrace bar are there to be sociable in. The bar is also a suitable place to enquire about a viticulture tour or to sample the wines produced on these very premises.

THE UPSIDE: They make wine and they let you camp, what more do you need?

THE DOWNSIDE: Popular with retired people, so noisy types needn't apply.

THE DAMAGE: For 2 people with a car and tent or caravan it's €15.75 per night. Extra adults cost €3.85 per night

THE FACILITIES: The washroom consists of four showers and toilets, and there are two outdoor showers (hoses in the garden) to wash off grass. There's the wooden dining area and bar, a washing machine and a mini garden terrace.

FOOD AND DRINK: Three times a week the owners prepare four-course meals for €15 (they charge students less). They really try to spoil their guests by mixing up Dutch and French cooking to produce unseen, novel recipes. Their own white wine, Vin de Pays des Côtes de Gascoigne ranges between €3.85 and €5.85 per bottle.

FAMILY FUN: Have a simple, inexpensive day at Condom park, along the Baise River. You get to relax in shady areas and the kids get to play with French children at a large playground with slides and climbing frames. The park is signposted in the town.

TREAT YOURSELF: To a beginner's lesson flying a small aircraft or opt for a less-demanding ride in one, 12 miles (20 km) away in Nogaro at the Aéroclub du Bas Armagnac (00 33 5 62 08 80 82; www.aeronogaro.com).

GETTING THERE: The N124 from Toulouse takes you nearly all the way there; you join the D931 towards Eauze where you take the D43 to Castelnau d'Auzan.

OPEN: May–Sept.

IF IT'S FULL: The *Cool Camping* site of La Brouquère in Gondrin is nearby (see p148).

Domaine Le Poteau, 32440 Castelnau d'Auzan | t | 00 33 5 62 29 25 95 | w | www.le-poteau.com

LF-RZ-67

la brouquère

'Arrive as a guest, leave as a friend.' With only six pitches going at any one time the owners of La Brouquère haven't set themselves too difficult a motto to aspire to. Here in Gers, midway between the Mediterranean and the Atlantic, La Brouquère sits in a deliciously untouristy region of France. So, unless you become firm friends with a local farmer or spend dawn 'til dusk exploring the countryside, you'll definitely leave having got to know Sonja and Wouter a whole lot better.

One thing sure to leave an impression on you is their passion. Relocating from Holland a few years ago, the couple restored an old winery using its original stone for the structure of their gorgeous bijou home: with bright blue shutters, a view of rolling hills and, from June, blossoming sunflowers. There's a pleasant drive past vineyards to get here and an intimate camping vibe that greets you on arrival. All of La Brouquère's USPs share equal pride of place: the little swimming pool – actually, it's not much bigger than a hot tub, but it'll cool you down on sunny days; the terraced patio; the views and the house are all vividly enchanting.

In medieval times, this part of France fell slap bang in the middle of crossfire between English and French armies based west of here at Bordeaux and at Toulouse, further south. Nowadays, Gers is an unspoilt, rural landscape peppered with green vineyards and yellow sunflower fields. Its remoteness enables workmen to travel freely about their daily business, which for many is the production of *foie gras* and Armagnac. Such low tourist traffic is a red flag for bullish travellers, for whom La Brouquère makes an appealing, peaceful holiday choice.

The French eat duck like the Brits eat chicken. You're likely to find *foie gras* (duck or goose liver pâté) and *magret de canard* (duck breast) on menus all over France. To taste alternative recipes you might like to waddle along to La Ferme du Cassou, which offers a tour of the production of pâté followed by a sampling session of duck omelettes, sausages, tarts and jams. You can, of course, duck out (sorry) of this gamey feast and instead opt for La Brouquère's home-cooked food. A veritable smorgasbord – Indonesian, Indian, Greek, Italian and Swiss meals all feature; and vegetarians are well catered for. Whenever you feel the need to work up an appetite for their *table d'hôte* evening *menus*, or work them off, there's a circular swimming pool only 2 miles (3 km) away in the village of Gondrin.

You have the choice of camping in the garden or on wilder land further back, with lots of space to lie spread-eagle on blankets whilst you peruse Sonja's comprehensive bumper-packed folder of local activities. The shared facilities are excellent. Or, if you're a product junkie who always ends up leaving your favourite shampoo in the shower, think about hiring the campsite's private bathroom – but book well in advance, it's a popular feature.

Pre-order bread and croissants the day before and in the morning chow down on your breakfast in full view of uninterrupted Armagnac landscape. Vineyards are visible from your tent in one direction and, in the other, rolling hills separate you from the charming provincial town of Condom, a 10-minute drive away.

Sonja and Wouter believe that the Gers is the best region in all of France, that the locally produced wine is better than any Bordeaux and that 'don't worry' is your password to a happy stay at La Brouquère. And if, after a few days exploring or relaxing, you begin to agree with those opinions, you'll have the perfect excuse to return – and visit your new-found friends.

THE UPSIDE: Tiny, friendly campsite; wine and Armagnac brandy virtually on tap. Hic.

THE DOWNSIDE: There are only six pitches, so hurry, hurry, hurry.

THE DAMAGE: €7–9.20 per person per night (it's slightly less for children). You can rent your own bathroom for a small charge. The owners also rent a *gîte* that sleeps 5 and is nestled amongst the vineyards, from €250 a week.

THE FACILITIES: Six 200 sq. m pitches for tents and cars. Two showers, four toilets and one private shower room with a toilet. No fires are allowed. If you have to stay in touch there's wi-fi, and you can re-freeze blocks for your cool box. Plus, there's a small children's playground and a *boules* pitch.

FOOD AND DRINK: Gondrin's La Ferme du Cassou hosts four duck-tasting sessions a week (00 33 5 62 29 15 22; www.fermeducassou.com). If you like brandy, and the best place to try it is Château de Cassaigne (00 33 5 62 28 04 02), which offers free tours and tastings, then a decent bottle of Armagnac will set you back around €25.

FAMILY FUN: The tiny museum in Lupiac commemorates the birthplace of d'Artagnan, who fought alongside the three musketeers; it's worth a look. The Thursday market at Eauze is a must-see and, closer to home (turn right at the end of the road) there's a modest paint-balling site in a stack of hay bales (00 33 6 74 52 16 87).

TREAT YOURSELF: Ok, we know it's not environmentally friendly, but if you want to make like Formula One's Lewis Hamilton, then the race circuit 30 minutes away at Nogaro might appeal. One-day courses start at €340. (Circuit Paul Armagnac, Nogaro; 00 33 5 62 09 02).

GETTING THERE: The village is located on the D931 between Condom and Eauze (31 miles/ 50 km) from Auch and Agen.

OPEN: June–Sept.

IF IT'S FULL: Head for the nearby *Cool Camping* site of Domaine Le Poteau (see p146), which has its own vineyard.

Camping La Brouquère, 32330 Gondrin	t	00 33 5 62 29 19 44	w	www.brouquere.com

les ormes

Can't make it to Africa this year? Then make Les Ormes your next choice. Six years ago, two Dutch couples spied a gap in the travel market, threw in their office jobs and began importing desert tents from South Africa for their newly acquired plot of land in the Lot-et-Garonne. Inspired by a luxury tent hotel they spotted in Tanzania, their quest was to create an authentic but comfortable camping experience aimed at thirtysomethings who may have enjoyed childhood holidays under canvas, and now want to replicate the experience with their own brood. And with a few extra creature comforts.

Twenty-five desert tents are spaciously plotted within a forest of *ormes* (elm trees) – in a setting not too dissimilar to the jungles of the Congo...with a little imagination. There are various configurations to choose from: the Gibsons have large terraced awnings, four of them also have tree-tents for the kids; the Takla-Makan is a tent for two, with a sleeping and a living area; whilst the Mojaves have stunning valley views. All tents have hip interior touches, comfortable spring beds and fresh linen. They look very chic indeed, but for an even more impressive water-cooler story to share back home, stay in the 360° rotating Tournesol chalet. Built on a ring with wheels, you turn it to face the sun, or move it back into the shade when it gets too hot. And if you think that's classy, then the owners' next project – floating chalets on a man-made pond – is sure to blow us all away.

For the traditional tenters amongst us there are 90 spacious tent pitches up for grabs amongst hilly and flat fields. It's a good idea to camp as near to the wonderful bottle-green lake, which offers boating and carp fishing, next to the candy-coloured swimming pool, but as far away from the huge, central facility block as you can. A bastion of many a French campsite, rows of changing rooms and cubicles act as a bustling crossroads to the campsite's various destinations, so it gets a bit noisy there early morning.

Off site, Dordogne's buzzy town of Bergerac half an hour away boasts 12 appellations of red, white and rosé and dozens of winemakers who'll be keen to welcome your custom. Once the key port for distributing wine to the UK, a role since passed on to Bordeaux, you can now find good-value for your money here. Take your time to hunt down your favourite taste by touring the Bergerac Wine Route (La Route des Vins de Bergerac), a map of picturesque vineyards against backdrops of castles, paper mills and walled villages. Ok, so it would take you a while to complete, but who's in a rush?

The nearby village of Saint-Étienne de Villeréal isn't as remarkable as the many beauties lying further north in the Dordogne. On the bright side, this makes the area feel less like a tourist trap (with less traffic!) and more an unspoilt slice of real France. Many villages and markets can be explored for tasty food to cook back at your desert tent – maybe you'll find some South African cocoa beans to whip up a thick French–African hot chocolate recipe.

Your time in this laid-back base is very much your own. And whilst it may not quite have the exotic safari style of a true African camp, it feels a continent away from the larger, commercial campsites that can be spotted clogging up watering holes across France.

THE UPSIDE: Comfortable camping and safari style.

THE DOWNSIDE: The site is huge (over 60 acres) and takes an hour to walk around.

THE DAMAGE: The 90 tent pitches are €6–13 per night, depending on season. Off-season, over-50s are €13 and families €20 all-in. Weekly hire of basic tents and the quirky Tournesol is between €285 and €485. The safari-style tents start about €325 and go up to €875 for the top-of-the-range Takla-Makan.

FACILITIES: Everything you need: a barn restaurant, reception, tennis, table tennis, *boules*, fishing, volleyball, swimming pool, lake, small animal farm, a swimming pool Zanzi-Bar and nearby, a 18-hole golf course.

FOOD AND DRINK: Take the D660 to Château Les Merles (00 33 5 53 63 13 42; www.lesmerles.com) in Mouleydiar for eight-course banquets in the restaurant or less in the bistro. In an area famous for sweet dessert white wine produced from a mixture of Sauvignon and Semillon grapes *the* place to taste it is Château Monbazillac (Route de Mont-de-Marsan, 24240 Monbazillac; 00 33 5 53 63 65 00).

TREAT YOURSELF: To a Michelin-starred meal. Chef Vincent Arnould earned his star at Le Vieux Logis, Tremolat (00 33 5 53 22 80 06; www.vieux-logis.com).

GETTING THERE: Ryanair fly to Bergerac, from where it's a 40-minute drive to the campsite. Take the N21 from Villeneuve or Bergerac and turn off at the D2 towards Saint-Étienne de Villeréal, the campsite is well signposted from there.

OPEN: Late-Apr–Sept.

IF IT'S FULL: Campsite Le Moulin de David is just up the road at Monpazier. It has a pool complex with a lake, waterfalls and slides, which will keep the kids occupied (00 33 5 53 22 65 25; www.moulin-de-david.com).

Camping Les Ormes, 47210 Saint Étienne de Villéreal

t 00 33 5 53 36 60 26 w www.campinglesormes.com

le petit lion

When Dorothy and Toto set off along the Yellow Brick Road on their way to Oz, first they walk through a landscape of rich colourful cornfields. And you, too, will get the feeling that you're 'not in Kansas anymore' as you cruise towards Le Petit Lion from the tiny village of Gurat. For a start, on either side of the road are shoulder-high fields of sunflowers and maize. Then, there's the odd scarecrow, which may make you double take – just to make sure he's not changing the way he's pointing or smiling brainlessly at you. And when you get to Le Petit Lion you'll think that the only thing missing is the tin man.

Of course, this isn't Oz, nor is it the Yellow Brick Road. For a start the road isn't brick and the tarmac's black. But it's not a million metaphorical miles away, because this is one of the old pilgrim routes to Santiago de Compostela in Spain, where, it is claimed, lie the bones of the apostle St James. From medieval times there have been several different routes through France – starting from Paris, Vézelay, Le Puy and Arles – that slowly converge like tributaries of a river at the border with Spain, from whence pilgrims would make their way on foot all the way to Galicia. Nowadays, of course, pilgrims take things a little easier. Some drive, some cycle and those that do still walk parts of the route do so on the air-cushioned soles of popular brands of running shoe. But the end is the same and, as philosophers and therapists will tell you, it's not the destination but the journey that is the real deal.

Still, you've got to break the journey somewhere and a fair number of pilgrims – French, Dutch and German in the main – choose to do so at Le Petit Lion. So, don't be surprised to see people here lounging around with their feet up. Chances are they've deserved it.

The campsite is owned by a welcoming British couple, Mark and Stephanie Reed, who are always on hand primed with a bottle of Pineau des Charentes for the weary traveller. After a hard day on the road, it's a welcome tipple, a little like sherry but not the kind your aunt serves at Christmas. It's more the sort of thing you'll find youngsters sipping in hip French bars.

Outside, the campsite is fairly compact but the pitches are generously spread amongst some pretty fancy trees, such as walnut, cherry and hazelnut. It makes a change from the ubiquitous pines that shade many a French campsite. And if you fancy a break from the canvas there are also four trendy *campahuttes* (chalets made from red cedar wood) available for hire.

When it's time to hit the road again, there are plenty of historic sights in the vicinity. The nearest village, Gurat, has a 10th-century, flinty-stoned Gallo-Roman church, whilst the nearby town of Villebois-Lavalette has an impressive fortified *château* on top of a hill along with a classic French covered market – all timbered beams, burgundy roof tiles and no walls.

A little further north is the city of Angoulême, which is famous for a couple of curiosities. First is Le Circuit des Remparts, a classic car rally held every September around the city. It's not exactly Monte Carlo but you get the idea. There is also, rather bizarrely, an annual international comic strip festival held at the national comic strip museum – housed in an appropriately odd building of glass and stone on rue de Bordeaux that was once a Benedictine abbey and then a brewery. You really couldn't make it up. Well, I suppose you could...if you lived in the Emerald City and your name was the Wizard of Oz.

THE UPSIDE: A quiet site with wonderful trees and a spiritually uplifting clientele.

THE DOWNSIDE: It's not quite the Dordogne.

THE DAMAGE: A pitch plus car, caravan or camper is €5 per night plus €3 per adult. Under-7s are €2. Electricity is €3. Weekly hire of a *campahutte* is €300.

THE FACILITIES: Adequate, but not sparkling, amenities block with all the requisites (including disabled facilities). There are also two swimming pools, swings, table tennis and *boules* to keep you amused.

FOOD AND DRINK: There are free range eggs and fresh vegetables available from the site (and chestnuts when in season!) but this is a rural site a couple of miles from the nearest village so it's best to cater for yourself. Saturday is market day at Villebois-Lavalette.

FAMILY FUN: Go kayaking on the quiet waters of the beautiful town of Brantôme. It's known as the Venice of the Périgord and sits on a loop in the River Dronne. If kayaking sounds too strenuous for you, sit back and ply the river on the motor boat that leaves from Quai de Pavillion Renaissance.

TREAT YOURSELF: To a case of Pineau des Charentes. It makes a change from a case of claret and will give your aunt a surprise.

GETTING THERE: Head south from Angoulême on the D674. Take the D5 towards Villebois-Lavalette. Just short of the town, turn right onto a bypass road which joins the D17 heading south. At the garage in Gurat, turn left and follow the narrow road to a fork. Take the right-hand road and stay on it until you see the entrance to the campsite on your right.

OPEN: All year.

IF IT'S FULL: There's a smallish but decent municipal site (Camping Municipal, Le Pontis Sud Est, 24320 Vendoire; 00 33 5 53 90 37 74) nearby at Verteillac.

Le Petit Lion, 24320 Vendoire | t | 00 33 5 53 91 00 74 | w | www.lepetitlion.co.uk

CANOE - KAYAK

camping de l'îlot

With over 250 campsites in the Dordogne to choose from, why opt for Camping de L'îlot? For one thing, it'll beat having to fight for towel space during your morning swim, something you have to do at many of the more confined riverside spots in France. And the Auvézère river's 'beach', which is what the French tend to call their river banks at low tide, has its own lifeguard.

There's a reason why you won't be sharing your patch with all and sundry. Cubjac is a little out of the way for tourists to get to from the south, even by the Dordogne's usual long-winded standards. Which means that even if all the pitches at the campsite are booked – and it's such a scorcher of a day that the villagers are out swimming off their marathon lunches – you'll still have plenty of room to play frisbee along the water's edge.

L'îlot means 'small island' and Camping de L'îlot's pride is that it's flanked by a river on one side and a canal on the other (admittedly the canal is some way back from the site). You enter Cubjac over an elegant bridge from the south, then either walk over a little footbridge or take the second right to drive onto the campsite. It's a river bank location where gangs of ducks breeze downstream, gossiping with their friends under the main bridge like teenagers on a village night out. Idly watching them from the campsite's grassy slopes is a favoured pastime of many a camper here.

Monsieur Musitelli is a typical-looking Frenchman. And, you couldn't find a more accommodating host if you tried. Maybe his happiness is his islet. It never rains here, he claims; although, one look at the lush-green vegetation and you can see he's fibbing. His modest picture-postcard campsite is one heavily shaded by trees, with plenty of nooks and crannies that suit group bookings down to the ground.

Being in the centre of the village – the few shops are just behind the campsite – means that food is never far away. There's a baker, butcher, pharmacy, grocery store, post office, café and a market every Friday morning, all just a hop, jump and skip away from your tent. Actually, it's questionable whether anyone other than the shop-workers live here, it seems that sleepy a place.

Whenever you wish to up the tempo, the best plan would be to go horse riding locally or feel the wind in your hair further afield amongst the valleys of the Dordogne. Travel west to Rouffiac for one of the biggest leisure lakes in the Périgord area where you can swim (there is a larger sandy beach here, again with supervised bathing, plus options to windsurf, hire kayaks or go water-skiing). Otherwise, for a fill of culture then Périgueux, the capital of the Dordogne has a little. It's a city full of Gallo–Roman, Renaissance and Byzantine history; the old city on the west side of the town holds the most interest for a stroll.

It depends how long a stay you're planning, but if the weather's good it's probably not worth leaving Cubjac's river banks until you're feeling truly revived and recharged. Anyway, you'd be doing the lifeguard a favour: hanging out with those ducks all day must get a bit lonesome.

THE UPSIDE: 'Beach' life, in a village, without the crowds.

THE DOWNSIDE: It's a long drive to get to any other sights in the Périgord region.

THE DAMAGE: There are 50 pitches and 12 mobile homes (that sleep 4–6). A tent with 2 people costs from €9.40 per night.

THE FACILITIES: There are five basic showers, seven toilets, five wash basins and a washing machine; plus wi-fi Internet access in the café. Food-wise, they sell snacks, pizzas, steak and chips to fuel active pursuits including tennis, canoeing, volleyball, basketball and ping-pong. A small beach with a lifeguard, a baby corner and equipment for the disabled also feature.

FOOD AND DRINK: Goose gizzards, anyone? This Périgord delicacy, mostly found in salads, is served in many restaurants. Sorges, 8 miles (13 km) north, is home to a truffle museum, truffle-hunting country walks (depending on the season) and the Auberge de la Truffe, with set *menus* that cost up to €120 (00 33 5 53 05 02 05; www.auberge-de-la-truffe.com). A good family choice is L'Étang du Coucou, where there's a swimming and fishing lake with a restaurant and it promotes the occasional jazz music evening too (24390 Hautefort; 00 33 5 53 51 96 14).

FAMILY FUN: Strike out for the Snook Bowl Palace bowling centre (La Feuilleraie, 24750 Trelissac; 00 33 5 53 08 55 68) just outside Périgueux in Trelissac 9 miles (15 km) away.

TREAT YOURSELF: To an overnight horse trek. Yes, you read that right. For €190 you get two five-hour rides around the caves north of Les Eyzies, plus picnics and accommodation (Ferme du Fonluc, 24620 Les Eyzies de Tayac; 00 33 5 53 35 30 06; www.fonluc.com).

GETTING THERE: East of Périgueux the D5 will take you into the village, the site is on the left on the river bank. From the south, get off either side of the A89 and onto the D6089 that runs parallel with it, turning north on the D68. Crawl along country roads, over the bridge at Cubjac, second right into the site and *vous êtes arrivé*.

OPEN: Apr–Sept.

IF IT'S FULL: The *Cool Camping* site at Le Capeyrou (see p164) is over an hour's drive away, but if you'd prefer somewhere nearer to Cubjac or Périgueux, then off the D5 at Boulazac is Camping de Barnabé (rue des Bains, 24750 Boulazac; 00 33 5 53 53 41 45; www.barnabe-perigord.com), with a 1930s bar, a landscaped garden and mini-golf.

Camping de L'îlot, 24640 Cubjac	t	00 33 5 53 05 39 79	w	www.domainelafaurie.com

le capeyrou

Are you sitting comfortably? Then we'll begin. Once upon a time in a land far, far away was a beautiful campsite. And perched high on a cliff above that campsite was a fairytale castle. Every evening the magic dragon who lived in the castle sprinkled magic sparkle-dust on the campsite below, which made everybody very, very happy.

OK, so we made up the bit about the dragon and the magic sparkle-dust, but Le Capeyrou does indeed stand in the shadows of the beautiful 12th-century Château de Beynac.

The Dordogne may be renowned for its feudal castles, but Beynac is its most fairytale-inspiring one. An early nickname 'Satan's Ark' (earned by the brutal actions of its baron owners) belies its unquestionable beauty; a charming scramble of pointy turrets and fudgy edges, all seemingly ready to tumble from its precarious perch at the slightest sneeze.

The castle lords over the striking village of Beynac-et-Cazenac, whose narrow medieval streets and ancient houses became the setting for the Juliette Binoche and Johnny Depp film *Chocolat*. Even today, its manicured, toy-town glamour feels a bit like the set of a period drama. Climbing the steep, cobbled hill to the fortified walls – 150 metres above ground level – brings you to a majestic view of the neighbouring villages of Castelnaud, Fayrac and Marqueyssac.

A young French–Dutch husband-and-wife team run their aesthetically astute campsite with 120-pitches broken up by hedgerows, along the northern edge of the River Dordogne, under the castle's watchful eye. Well-tended lawns and a civilised mood dominate the atmosphere. Even though this is an area choking with sporting activities, riverside tranquillity is available in buckets, leaving you free to plan an itinerary as sedentary or as vigorous as you wish.

Whilst a holiday in the Dordogne really does benefit from having your own wheels – there's not a lot of public transport – at Le Capeyrou there's so much on your doorstep that you'll get by just fine without. Cycling, fishing, shopping, hot-air ballooning and, of course, walking, are all easy to organise. You can also get taken up river to Cénac-et-Saint-Julien, from where you'll paddle canoes past five different castles, ending up at a finishing line just yards from your tent.

Six miles (9.5 km) away is the lovely town of Sarlat-la-Canéda, the capital of Périgord Noir (Périgord is in the Aquitaine region and is split into black, green, white and purple divisions). Not that there's anything remotely *noir* about Sarlat; it's a delightful town of preserved limestone edifices and pedestrianised alleys. English-speaking voices are ubiquitous, you might feel like you're on a tourist trail, but we defy you to not join in with the collective gasp that every corner turn elicits.

There are many great places to hang out, too. In the interests of research, we sampled the cocktails at the main square's Bar des Isles and can happily report that they are excellent. There's also the French-run Le Pub, where you can sup pints in a courtyard. Once you've whet your appetite, masses of restaurants compete to seat you on their terrace within the centre's mythical caramel-coloured walls.

Le Capeyrou has a bar, too; you'll find it inside the location's centrepiece, a converted barn. The beamed saloon contains a huge furnace fire, high chairs and tables, which together with the outside patio turns into the social setting for weekly meals. There's also a pool table, wi-fi and a few stuffed bookshelves. Outdoors you'll find ping-pong tables and a stylish swimming pool with an adjoining paddling pool to keep the kids' splash count low. So, all in all, the perfect place to live happily ever after. The End.

THE UPSIDE: Castle-gazing on grassy lawns transports you to your own private fairytale.

THE DOWNSIDE: Bumper-to-bumper traffic in high summer along the windy roads can be unbearable.

THE DAMAGE: Two people with a tent costs €14.20–17.90 per night, less for under-7s.

THE FACILITIES: Water and electricity points, swimming pool, table tennis, volleyball, mini supermarket, showers, toilets and a washing machine. The occasional dancing night keeps the teens happy.

FOOD AND DRINK: The Dordogne is all about *foie gras* and truffles. The truffles are harvested December to March, so you'll find them at their freshest and tastiest in the winter. Otherwise, conserved or more inferior, cheaper truffles (by no means the legendary 'black diamond') can be found during the summer.

FAMILY FUN: Underwater tunnels and tropical fish await just minutes away at the Aquarium du Périgord Noir (24260 Le Bugue Vézère; 00 33 5 53 07 10 74; www.parc-aquarium.com).

TREAT YOURSELF: To an evening in the romantic Jardins de Marqueyssac (see picture, right). Every Thursday in July and August this garden is lit by candles as easy-listening music plays out of the bar (Jardins de Marqueyssac, 24220 Vezac; 00 33 5 53 31 36 36; 7pm–12midnight, last entry 11pm; www.marqueyssac.com).

GETTING THERE: Head towards Sarlat. Beynac-et-Cazenac is 5 miles (8 km) southwest, off the D57. Coming in from Bergerac, you're driving alongside the River Dordogne. The route might not look too windy on the map but expect the journey to take a couple of hours.

PUBLIC TRANSPORT: Fly or take an SNCF train to Bordeaux and then a three-hour train ride to Sarlat. Or fly to Bergerac, it takes two hours by train from there.

OPEN: Easter–Sept.

IF IT'S FULL: Thirty minutes west on the D703/D25 in Le Buisson de Cadouin is Camping du Pont de Vicq (00 33 5 53 22 01 73) which has fabulous grassy pitches just a stone's throw from the river's edge.

Camping Le Capeyrou, 24220 Beynac-et-Cazenac	t	00 33 5 53 29 54 95	w	www.campinglecapeyrou.com

camping de l'ouysse

Camping à la ferme offers all the rural escapism you could possibly need to leave the daily grind behinds and go rustic. But it takes a special family to throw open their gates to welcome a public wired from work and travel. Fortunately, the couple at this particular idyll have unlimited patience and also possess a gentle demeanour, which they deploy whenever they're under interrogation. So many questions need answering. And some people, with all their idiosyncratic charm, sure ask lots of them before easing themselves into the slower-paced swing of things. The ace card that always disarms new arrivals, unravelling their stress like a frayed seam, is the response to 'where do we camp?'. With an outstretched arm, 'anywhere' is the reply. Elated eyes sweep the lie of the land, down across an orchard of plum, apple and cherry trees, down to a river and onwards into a field that seems to go on forever.

Your next dilemma could last a while: should you go for a shady riverside spot or one in the meadow, or opt for complete solitude at the furthest point from the farmhouse, beside the rugged mountain rock face? Because of strict legislation, only 12 tents can be pitched here at any time, which is good news for campers who love their privacy. Although, some people can take that to the extreme: the owners tell a story of one gentleman who trekked the 700 metres to the edge of the field where he camped for a week. They didn't see him again until it was time for him to leave. As odd as that may or may not be, you get the picture – there's lots of space in the place, which makes it difficult to disturb either farmer or neighbour.

The dark-green River Ouysse flows past the farmhouse under a leafy tunnel of walnut and poplar trees, on its journey to the village of Lacave where it eventually joins the Dordogne. Crossing the tightrope bridge over this water places you at the start of fantastic hikes through woods and fields. The best is the one that follows the river to the 12th-century working watermill at Cougnaguet and on through the Alzou valley towards the spectacular fortified village Rocamadour. The medieval stone atop the sheer cliff here has made it one of the most visited villages in France.

Take a couple of days off before psyching yourself up for the steep road to Cales, a village on a hill-top plateau. Lunch at one of the pretty eateries will taste so good, partly from knowing it's downhill all the way back. In the other direction is the village of Lacave, where many tourists come each year to explore the caves. *Grottes* are familiar all over France but this one's a little bit different, instead of a boat you travel deep into the rock by electric train to experience its stalagmites, caves and underwater lakes.

Camping de l'Ouysse has a few water toys at your disposal. From the site, a kayak and a couple of canoes can simply be lifted into the river, which makes a change from signing up for one of the many organised excursions you get around the Dordogne. You're in the Lot region, an hour from the bustle of Sarlat-la-Canéda, but a million miles away from the thousands of tourists that go there. It's just you, and a dozen other tents – maximum!

THE UPSIDE: The space. Lovely.

THE DOWNSIDE: Unusually, they don't sell any produce here: it's a 10-minute drive to the shops to get fresh breakfast bread yourself.

THE DAMAGE: Prices per night for an adult €4, and children €2, with tents. A tiny, almost-forgotten-looking caravan (sleeps 2) costs €8 per person per night.

THE FACILITIES: Two outdoor facilities huts complete with a BBQ, two showers and a toilet.

FOOD AND DRINK: A bargain five-course set menu at the Ferme Auberge Calvel (Le Bougayrou; 00 33 5 65 37 87 20) starts at €13 and can be eaten on long wooden tables in the garden. The Friday market at Souillac sells local specialities such as *foie gras*, walnut oil and lots more.

FAMILY FUN: Les Grottes de Lacave (00 33 5 65 32 28 28; www.grottes-de-lacave.com) is the nearest non-walking/cycling/eating activity. Failing that, feeding the monkeys with popcorn at the 50-acre Monkey Forest near Rocamadour will be as much of a treat for you as it is for them (L'Hospitalet, 46500 Rocamadour; 00 33 5 65 33 62 72; www.la-foret-des-singes.com).

TREAT YOURSELF: To a night out at the Pont de l'Ouysse – a decadent one-star Michelin restaurant in Lacave (46200 Lacave; 00 33 5 65 37 87 04; www.lepontdelouysse.fr).

GETTING THERE: Port de Souillac, just south of where the N20 joins the D804 taking heavy traffic west alongside the Dordogne, is the D43 corner turn to Lacave. Before you reach the village you'll see signs on your right for Calès. The site is on a left-hand bend at the foot of the hill.

OPEN: Apr–Sept.

IF IT'S FULL: Past Lacave village, the authentically French restaurant Ferme Auberge Calvel also has eight camping spaces (for details see FOOD AND DRINK).

Camping de l'Ouysse, Le Bourgnou, 46200 Lacave	t	00 33 5 65 32 63 01	e	d.vincent4@wannadoo.fr

camping pyrénées natura

With 'luxury' and 'comfort' two heavily bandied buzzwords of recent times, it might seem inconceivable that anywhere could rival the architecture of the hippest boutique hotels. But whereas such grandeur may boast unbeatable neon skylines or the latest in spa fashion, the Pyrénées safeguard something no money can buy – the Great Outdoors. Mesmerising and spiritual, the mountainous terrain with all its seasonal temperaments and wildlife offers an experience that humbles humans to their very core.

If, however, you like deluxe comforts to complement your concord with nature, then Camping Pyrénées Natura is just up your street. Even the facilities are a breath of fresh air. The owners never once rested on their laurels, and they've been going for 10 years. But then you don't become a French 4-star establishment without some effort, and Pascal and Valerie Ruysschaert have devoted their time to creating the kind of campsite they spent their lives looking for, but never found.

In 1995, they bought and restored a 19th-century barn to house a games room, library and bar, where Pascal mixes up a mean Pyrénées Natura house cocktail – a potent wine and Armagnac concoction. Next, they built a sauna-solarium, a soundproof music room with a top-notch sound system and a little shop to sell local produce.

The Ruysschaerts decided against a swimming pool, seeing it as superfluous and just plain noisy. Anyway, there are plenty of watery encounters possible in the many lakes in the area, and Arrens-Marsous 3 miles (5 km) away has a heated outdoor pool. In the other direction is the closest town – Argelès-Gazost: a friendly place to stock up on necessities, where cries of '*Bonne journée*' seem to resound out of the shops with regular frequency.

Estaing is a recently built village – constructed in the Second World War as a stopgap for evacuees crossing the border into Spain. The current population of just 60 people means that should you hanker for company, then there are plenty of characters around, it's just they tend to be of the feathered variety. Isards, marmots, golden eagles, griffons, Egyptian vultures and the rare (3-metre wing-span) lammergeyer all thrive here. Valerie has her own Dutch bantams, which proudly parade their bright headdresses around campus, whilst Pascal's alarm clock has a birdsong ring; it goes off at 5am when one of them will get to work making breakfast bread to sell in the shop.

It's a bewitching drive up the mountain, passing streams, valleys, cows and donkeys. It's a shame you can't bottle this air, you could make a killing with it back in Blighty. On arrival, campers and mobile homes are directed to the right of the campsite, on a field set back from the barn. Along the breadth of the site are two rows of chalets. You may be so close to your neighbours that you can see them intimately through the windows, but on the plus side, the units are replaced with fresh models every few years (and anyway, you can always pull the curtains).

Pascal gives all new arrivals a sheet of activity suggestions. The hiking is good, the night hikes are particularly popular, and the fighting fit might like to cycle around the various *cols* (mountain passes). You can walk to Lac d'Estaing – it's just at the end of the road. A drive to the three Cirques – Troumouse, Gavarnie and Vignemale – will leave you feeling no bigger than a pinprick in comparison to these alpine basins, and about as significant. It's a campsite that lives up to its name; nature's booty is all that you should seek.

THE UPSIDE: A three-hour drive from Toulouse and you're camped up in the fresh mountain air.
THE DOWNSIDE: It gets ultra nippy at night in the mountains so stock up on warm camping gear.
THE DAMAGE: Two people with a tent (or caravan), car and electricity €15.50–24.50 per night, depending on the season. Under-8s €3.50 and an additional person €5.25.
THE FACILITIES: There's room for 60 tents, 30 mobile chalets and five motor homes. Ten showers, Internet, an evening snack bar selling pizzas or main dishes (such as *coq au vin* or rabbit in mustard, from €4.50), plus a library, ping-pong, pool table, telescopes and an auditorium.
FOOD AND DRINK: People don't come here to go out to eat, says Valerie, but they do recommend locally produced cheese. Pascal will escort you to watch the shepherds at work and to sample their goats' award-winning *chèvre*.
FAMILY FUN: Rafting in various spots around here is fun and furious; it costs between €25 and €65 per person for distances of 6–18 miles (10–30 km) (Gave de Pau, 2 avenue des Pyrénées, 65400 Argelès-Gazost; 00 33 5 62 97 06 06).
TREAT YOURSELF: Restaurant du Lac d'Estaing by the lake offers a *menu séduction*. The food and view lives up to its title, even if the white plastic chairs and orange awning are more basic.
GETTING THERE: Hire a car and drive via Lourdes to Argelès-Gazost. From Argelès-Gazost take the D918 up the mountain, passing Camping Le Caoussariou (see IF IT'S FULL) turning left for the D13 and right on to the D103 towards Lac d'Estaing. You'll see the signpost for the site, on your right.
OPEN: Mid-May–mid-Sept.
IF IT'S FULL: Camping Le Caoussariou (Route d'Alzun, 65400 Arcizans-Dessus; 00 33 5 62 97 09 11) is a wide, open farm with 25 pitches, open mid-June–mid-Sept. You pass it on the D918, by the D13 turning.

Camping Pyrénées Natura, Route du Lac, 6500 Estaing

t 00 33 5 62 97 45 44 w www.camping-pyrenees-natura.com

– VENTE –
oie Gras Confit Armagnac
Produits Artisanaux

ferme du plantier

If camping in a French family's back garden is your idea of camping heaven, then the log piles at the driveway to Ferme du Plantier are your pearly gates.

Monsieur Capdevielle spends his days working in his dad's farming business. Like many producers in this region, honey is their main trade. And, like farmers all over Europe, the Capdevielles choose to boost their income by opening their garden to campers during the summer months. Their gently sloping land with shady trees is well maintained and comfortably squeezes in a full house of 20 pitches. The best of which lie at the bottom edge of the garden overlooking the Argelès–Gazost valley, set above a narrow road where traffic is pretty much limited to the odd tractor.

You won't find any of the fancy amenities common to certified campsites here, but then at €10 a night for two people you'll be happy with a few swings and the neighbour's friendly ginger tom-cat as your no-frills entertainment. The idea is to wake up slowly in this chilled retreat and plan your day. One more energetic option is to follow the road to Salles, where you'll find Le Bourdalat, an equestrian centre that offers the jazzier alternative of ski-jöring as well as good old-fashioned horse riding lessons. A sport normally associated with snow, ski-jöring here means you wear roller skates and, harnessed behind a horse, race along at whatever speed the horse rider dictates. Not everyone's *tasse de thé*, for sure.

There's a little snack restaurant at the stables selling pasta, salads and pizzas (chicken curry pizza anyone?), which is just the ticket after a half-day's hack. Or, from the campsite you could trek to a table at the summery lime green room at the Auberge du Bergons for a classic French *plat du jour*, such as succulent honeyed duck.

Also accessible on foot is Pibeste, a natural reserve that takes two and a half hours to walk to, your reward being amazing views of the summits of the Pyrénées. For a shorter 45-minute ramble, follow the signs to Le Balandrau and continue into Argelès-Gazost, a sprightly cornerstone town at the door of the eastern Pyrénées.

For exploring further afield a car is really helpful. If you've never been to Lourdes, the 10-minute drive from the campsite is surely obligatory. To see such commercial success thriving ever since a 14-year-old girl first saw a vision of the Virgin Mary in 1858 is testament to the faith that religion inspires worldwide. Over 250 hotels accommodate seven million tourists each year, and the shops certainly sort the browsers from the pros when it comes to sifting through tat: bottled holy water is sold by the crate load and the Virgin Mary is stacked in every conceivable merchandising form. Lourdes is a friendly tourist spot, where kitsch consumerism and pizza restaurants prosper, but the sight of so many people arriving from all over the world in search of miracle water cures at the Sanctuary of Our Lady of Lourdes is quite humbling.

But whilst the masses congregate in Lourdes, the countryside around is blissfully free of crowds and ideal for some extended walking or cycling excursions. And like the faithful flocking to the town, we're grateful for minor miracles, too – we just happen to think that Ferme du Plantier is one of them.

THE UPSIDE: Chilled-out farm camping with valley views and plenty around to enjoy.

THE DOWNSIDE: Once the valley view pitches have been snapped up, you might look out of your tent and think you could be in anyone's back garden. The couple don't speak English, which is worth knowing as they only offer telephone bookings.

THE DAMAGE: €10 per night for 2 people.

THE FACILITIES: In terms of the numbers, there are 20 tents, three basic showers, three toilets, three basins, one disabled shower/toilet, a washing machine and washing area, and 20 electric hook-ups. A caravan for hire at the northern tip of the garden sleeps four.

FOOD AND DRINK: La Chantignerie (65400 chemin Peyre; 00 33 5 62 97 17 84) has an outdoor terraced restaurant, situated down a narrow cobbled pathway decorated with flower baskets. Also in Salles, follow the road right out of the campsite and turn first right, up a steep narrow hill to Auberge du Bergons (00 33 5 62 90 15 76). It looks like an English National Trust tearoom, but the French classics at this *bistro du pays* firmly remind you which country you're in.

FAMILY FUN: Horse riding at Le Bourdalat (00 33 5 62 97 16 58; www.centre-equestre-pyrenees.com) costs €14 for one hour or €24 for two. A family Aqua-Pass at Aquensis, below, is €36 (family pass is for two adults and one child, but note there is no admission to under-5s).

TREAT YOURSELF: To a spa visit. The spectacular Aquensis is a magnificent wooden architectural thermal spa with a sundeck, saunas, jacuzzis, hammams, a relaxation area, two big thermal pools with hydro-massage and an oriental tearoom. Get here at the beginning of your holiday to immediately unwind (rue Pont d'Arras, 65202 Bagnères-de-Bigorre; 00 33 5 62 95 86 95).

OPEN: Jun–Sept.

GETTING THERE: From Pau airport it's the D938/7 to Lourdes and a right onto the D821. Access Ouzous via the D102. From Toulouse use the A64, taking exit 14 on the D20, which leads to the D935 then the D927 to Lourdes. On the D821 towards Argelès-Gazost, there's the D102 slip road to Ouzous. After a few bends you'll see the campsite sign on a driveway on your right.

IF IT'S FULL: Try the quiet, rural Camping Le Soleil du Pibeste (65400 Agos Vidalos; 00 33 5 62 97 53 23; www.campingpibeste.com), which has 67 pitches and a swimming pool.

Ferme du Plantier, rue de l'Oulet, 65400 Ouzous | t | 00 33 5 62 97 58 01

tipis indiens

All small boys whoop like Red Indians at some stage of their infancy. Some boys don't leave it at a simple rain dance in the playground, and instead pursue their intrigue further. When, as a teenager, you're spending all your time knocking out native North American Indian arrowheads, you know your hobby has turned into an obsession. But that's OK, because later, when you open up your very own tipi village and see the delight of every visitor who comes, you know it was time well invested.

Francis Caussieu grew up here in the Barèges valley and spent a little time travelling abroad before inheriting two countryside barns on the outskirts of the little village of Gèdre. He decided to renovate them and hire them out as *gîtes* throughout the year. He did this whilst building himself a house further down the mountain at Esterre. There, sitting and watching the seasons unfold before him like a slow-motion nature programme, he reflected on a childhood spent tearing around mountains and watching spaghetti Westerns. Francis concluded that even if he was never going to be like Clint Eastwood or Burt Lancaster, he could still create his very own film set.

In January 2004, his search began for a local craftsman who could make tipis. In the Alpes de Hautes Provence region, Francis found one with a passion to match his own. Together they chose designs that were easy to assemble and pull apart; then, they set about the harder task of finding a logger who'd select the strong woods needed to create sturdy dwellings. By June 2006, just a month before their first visitors were due, Francis was the proud owner of six tipis.

Each construction has two double beds and a small sofa bed with thick, snug duvets, a wooden chest, a table and a few Indian artefacts thrown in for good measure. The tipis are extremely cosy because the beds take up most of the space. There's a homely barn where you could stash a few belongings, although you would be sharing these facilities with the other tipi guests. You can shower, cook, watch TV in front of a small furnace fire or eat at the dining table – enjoying the best of both worlds, camping like an Indian and dining like a king.

Most people prefer to be in sight of the mountains in the evenings and as night falls they'll stack up firewood, for a campfire singsong with their friends and neighbours. Aside from its immediate location, with stunning views of the Cirque de Troumouse, you're surrounded by a landscape alive with goats and marmots.

The village, Gèdre, has a pool, an ice-skating rink and a bob luge, which are all open during the summer holidays. The village is also blessed with some excellent eateries, the best of all being La Brèche de Roland, where you should make a reservation early on in your stay, as the beef *filet* with melted ewes' cheese sauce may well lure you back for seconds.

Outside of Gèdre you drive past gorgeous scenery. There's the ski station town of Luz-Saint-Sauveur in the north where riverside cafés are jollied by colourful street bunting. Then, further south at Gavarnie is the highest waterfall in France, a worldly wonder situated just before the French–Spanish border. If you visit at the right time, avoiding heavy traffic, you can park up and then walk into one of the best natural amphitheatres in Europe. It'll be hard not to do your best Red Indian war-whoop cry here, but we wouldn't advise you to go disturbing the deafening peace.

THE UPSIDE: You're high up the mountains with the goats, living like a Red Indian.

THE DOWNSIDE: Goats with their droppings and coughs can be a disconcerting wake-up call.

THE DAMAGE: Prices for tipis in July and August for 1 night cost €85, €195 for 3 nights and €490 per week. In May, June and September, the weekly rate drops to €330 (apart from the last week in June which is €390).

THE FACILITIES: One *gîte* is available to all tipi guests with TV, sofas, a kitchen with *fondue* and *raclette* sets, washing machine, iron and two shower rooms. Guests must bring their own sheets and pillowcases, or you can hire linen for €5 per bed. Cleaning is an optional €10 per tipi.

FOOD AND DRINK: La Boutique des Cirques in town (place de la Fontaine) sells all kinds of local produce and crafts. La Brèche de Roland (00 33 5 62 92 48 54) is the centrally located village steak specialist.

FAMILY FUN: The goats were bought especially to please tourists and the kids can't get enough of them. A five-minute drive down the mountain to Gèdre is an outdoor pool, an indoor ice-skating rink and a bob luge.

TREAT YOURSELF: To a sunrise walk into the amphitheatre of the border town Gavarnie – without a doubt it will render you speechless. Or book a balcony view room at Hôtel Vignemale (00 33 5 62 92 40 00; www.hotel-vignemale.com) so you can just open the curtains for a similar effect.

GETTING THERE: A very pretty drive, the D821 to Argelès-Gazost leads to the D921 through Gèdre. At the village end, turn right, then the first left towards Saussa. Passing Camping Les Tilleuls on your left, continue until you see a few car park spaces on the right, and just after that is a small 'Tipis' sign on your left. It's a steep drive down, and it was a rocky one last year, but Francis said he'd be laying a smoother surface in time for the new season.

PUBLIC TRANSPORT: The SNCF train station at Lourdes is 26 miles (43 km) away with a bus service to Luz-Saint-Sauveur. From there you could order a Taxi Caussieu (Francis' brother; 00 33 5 62 92 97 56). Tarbes-Lourdes-Pyrénées airport is 37 miles (60 km) away and Toulouse airport 135 miles (217 km) away, a three-hour drive.

OPEN: May–Sept.

IF IT'S FULL: A short distance back downhill is the *Cool Camping* site of Les Tilleuls (see p184).

Tipis Indiens, 8 rue des Carolins, 65120 Luz-Saint-Sauveur | t 00 33 5 62 92 90 51 | w www.tipis-indiens.com

COLORADO

les tilleuls

Generations of the Millet family are so consumed with catching up on their gossip, they barely glance at the new arrivals inching down the driveway towards their patio table. When they do notice you, they'll fix you with the friendliest of smiles. Could they really be so used to the voluminous valley vista stretching out beneath them, that their eyes are not permanently fixed on the horizon? Surely no amount of time would weary one's appreciation of such a spectacular sight.

The view below is a chocolate-box mountainscape revealing the extraordinary terrain of Campbielh, Coumély and le Cirque de Gavarnie, dotted with old stone houses like a random scattering of Lego bricks. The Millets understand that such a fortunate location should be shared to be fully enjoyed, and so for many years have been allowing campers to experience the views from their garden (1100 metres above sea level). What's more, campers don't have to fight to be first with a front row seat, as the garden has been divided into four tiered levels, which all look down over the hamlets. And high-season travellers might want to pitch under one of the few trees, as there's nowhere else to hide from the sun on this campsite.

Perching high up on this privileged ridge, you'll feel like a bird of prey surveying the scene below – and Les Tilleuls is the perfect place to build your nest.

THE UPSIDE: Cracking valley views.

THE DOWNSIDE: Cars are allowed on site next to the tents, which seems a shame, as the site would look even prettier without them.

THE DAMAGE: There are 25 pitches costing from €10.50 for 2 adults with a car.

THE FACILITIES: Next to the vegetable garden is a very modern and clean block containing four showers, a sink, a basin for washing clothes and five toilets. Pets are allowed.

FOOD AND DRINK: The artisan shop on the road heading into Gèdre from the north sells Fleur d'Amour, a sherry-type *apéritif 'pour rester amoureux'*, a bargain at €12 (La Tannière, Pragnères, 65120 Gèdre; 00 33 5 62 92 49 11).

FAMILY FUN: A five-minute drive down the mountain to Gèdre is an outdoor pool, an indoor ice-skating rink (both open July and August) and a bob luge (opens mid-June).

TREAT YOURSELF: To a helicopter ride with Pyrénées Copt'Air (Jean-Philippe Duprat, Pyrénées Copt'Air, 64230 Poey-de-Lescar; 00 33 5 59 68 65 19). A 15–20-minute aerial view of the mountains and lakes costs from €120 for two people. The drive back north towards Argelès-Gazost to Hautacam will take less than an hour, but in good weather it's a scenic route you'll not tire of.

GETTING THERE: Follow the D821 to Argelès-Gazost then the D921 through Gèdre. At the village end, turn right, then first left towards Saussa. Follow the road and keep a look out for the almost hidden left turn down to Camping Les Tilleuls.

PUBLIC TRANSPORT: The SNCF train station at Lourdes is 26 miles (43 km) away with a bus service to Luz-Saint-Sauveur. Tarbes-Lourdes-Pyrénées airport is 37 miles (60 km) away or Toulouse airport 135 miles (217 km) is a three-hour drive away.

OPEN: Mid-May–mid-Sept.

IF IT'S FULL: The *Cool Camping* site of Tipis Indiens (see p180) further up the mountain has tipis for hire. If all else fails, the family on the other side of the road from Les Tilleuls allows campers on their tiny garden ledge. The facilities are pretty poor but it's cheap, from €4 a night for two people.

Camping Les Tilleuls, Saussa, 65120 Gèdre; t 00 33 5 62 92 48 92; e millet.rosalie@wanadoo.fr

belrepayre trailer park

Perry looks like a clown. He has the voluminous nose and wide expression, plus those side tufts of hair that you usually associate with clown wigs (the ones with the bald patches on top). So you won't be surprised to learn that he's a semi-retired circus performer who, in fact, worked for the industry's renowned impresario Gerry Cottle. He's the son of a legendary actor, he'll pull insightful quips out of his hat during general chit-chat and he owns a life size collection of London Transport memorabilia. But best of all, he's a creative genius who, together with his wife, has pulled off what for most would be like a pie-in-the-sky dream – Europe's first Airstream trailer park.

How does a son follow in the footsteps of the late Michael Balfour, a regular feature on British TV drama and comedy in the 1960s and later a star of many big-budget Hollywood movies? In Perry's case, you don't; you jump in with both oversized clown feet and form a father-and-son touring clown troupe – the Hazzards. Michael, Perry and his brother toured their theatrical gang show all over the UK in between acting assignments, travelling as a family in a 90-year-old caravan; then later on, when Perry had his own brood, they upgraded to a double-decker bus. If anything ever influenced Perry's life path, it was growing up amongst illustrious acting circles that ranged from Saturday matinee actors the Children's Film Foundation to the truly slapstick performers, the *Carry On* crew.

Living in the 1970s also made a mark, one that Perry never wanted to wash off. With his dad's advice – to always stay either one step ahead or a few steps behind fashion – ringing in his ears, Perry and his wife Coline put down roots and set about transforming an idyllic spot in the Ariège foothills of the Pyrénées into a themed trailer park. A novelty concept with incredible mileage, you could call it fashionable, but pioneering would be more accurate.

Over the past two decades the couple have amassed a collection of 15 Airstreams, restoring each one then kitting them out in retro fabrics and paraphernalia unearthed at flea markets. The model names of trailers are determined by their size, and, aside from an Airstream diner, which they stumbled across under the Eiffel Tower and turned into the Apollo bar, all their vehicles hail from America. They found a 1972 Sovereign in a nudist camp in Florida, a 1970s Tradewind model in New Mexico and a rare 1950s Silver Streak Clipper in Arizona.

BONNYTON
Canellese

CAFE
Airstream

Perry likens being inside an Airstream to being in the womb; designed like a capsule they make people feel safe and cosy. The interiors are truly wah-wah: all swirly patterns, knitted cushions and retro crockery. As well as a tiny bathroom, kitchen and wardrobes, each one has a black-and-white TV, an 8-track music system, a video player (ours came with a tape of *The Avengers*) and a mini garden with a fringed umbrella and sunloungers. BelRepayre's strong seventies theme is heightened with retro bunting and artistic touches all over the site, particularly in the Apollo bar-disco room. People really trip back in time here. Some guests bring 1970s clothes: floral or Hawaiian shirts, full skirts and flares are *de rigueur*. Perry dresses up when he turns into DJ Bobby Lotion to spin seminal New York or Italian disco along with chart-topping hits of the decade. He reckons people lose 35 years here. Which if true, really would leave some of us feeling deliciously ga-ga.

THE UPSIDE: Step back to the seventies at this unique retro caravan park. Cool, man.

THE DOWNSIDE: Turning up in your battered Rover and parking it next to a trailer might, rather embarrassingly, spoil the look.

THE DAMAGE: Airstream trailers, vintage caravans and campers (retro tents preferred please). A pitch and 2 people €18–27 per night. BelRepayre's Airstream hire costs from €74 a night to €550 a week (sleep up to 4). Extra charges for sheets, towels, dressing gowns and cleaning.

THE FACILITIES: There's lots: sauna, yoga room, ping-pong, badminton, bike tracks, outdoor cinema screen, DJ bar, evening food (high season only), a small shop selling organic produce, hot tub and communal showers. And Perry's son might perform a few magic tricks for you.

FOOD AND DRINK: Mirepoix has an exemplary farmer's market every Monday on place du Maréchal Leclerc. For something a bit more upmarket, head for the fabulous restaurant Le Comptoir Gourmand (Cours Maréchal de Mirepoix; 00 33 5 61 68 19 19), where you can feast on mussels to monkfish in a converted barn before stocking up on regional produce in their deli.

FAMILY FUN: This is really a playground for the grown-ups, but as Perry says, he welcomes *tout le monde* 'as long as they're nice'. Rambles through the bordering Bélène Forest should burn off some energy. Else notch up a gear and burn some rubber at the go-kart track near Carcassonne (00 33 4 68 25 67 07; www.winkart.fr).

TREAT YOURSELF: To a hot tub in view of the snow-capped mountains, followed by a massage then share a bottle of champagne under the stars (€30 for tub for two, massage €20–90).

GETTING THERE: It's near Mirepoix. Once your booking's confirmed you'll receive full directions. This secretive approach prevents curious tourists from interrupting everyone's privacy. Fly to Carcassonne, Pamiers or Toulouse then hire a car or Perry may even be able to pick you up from the airport. Or, if you arrive in your own classic car you'll get a 10% discount.

OPEN: End-Apr–Sept.

IF IT'S FULL: On the D625 from Mirepoix to Benaix you'll find Camping Le Mathibot (00 33 5 61 01 86 36), a simple six-pitch field behind a farm.

BelRepayre Airstream & Retro Camping, Near Mirepoix

	t	00 33 5 61 68 11 99	w	www.airstreameurope.com

val d'aleth

It seems incredible that for a relatively small village, Alet-les-Bains has so much going on inside its medieval walls. How many villages do you know that have a thermal spa, a *boulodrôme*, forest tree-walking, a casino with piano bar, a mini-stadium and a water sports centre for rafting and canoeing, as well as hot-air balloon trips and vineyards in close proximity? Not forgetting, a niche little campsite from where you can enjoy it all.

On the river bank of the Aude, Val d'Aleth is run by a couple originally from Surrey. Their 14-year-old campsite flourishes in a fine-looking backyard with space for 37 pitches. It may be in its teens but it's a well-developed project, perfectly positioned next to the remains of a 12th-century city wall and abbey. A single path runs either side of a middle row of trees where flowerpots have been placed for extra mojo. Either side of the paths are the pitches. It's a tough call deciding whether to go for a riverside spot or pitch in the shadow of medieval stone turrets.

Alet (pronounced Alette)-les-Bains sits between Limoux and Quillan, hugged by mountains. Once a walled city with its own bishop and cathedral, it's ecclesiastical legacy is the ruined abbey (the one flanking the campsite). The town's medieval square is surrounded by overhanging, half-timbered houses, including one that locals will tell you was once inhabited by the famous prophetic Nostradamus. Home to 500 villagers, Alet-les-Bains comes alive in the summer months when fêtes and dancing troupes pass through. A spa throws open its doors in May and a swimming pool filled with local mineral water – which sounds rather decadent – opens in June.

Val d'Aleth is just a 30-minute drive from Carcassonne, which makes it an easy escape for a long weekend. However, people do travel here from as far afield as Slovakia, New Zealand, Poland and probably the Home Counties to join the usual mix of French, Belgium, Dutch and British who camp regularly in France. So anything goes.

When you leave the campsite and follow the road up and around to the right, you've got a wonderful panoramic of the whole village. There's so much to do in the area, from discovering villages further west or the coastal towns east on the Mediterranean, exploring grottoes or disco dancing in

Limoux. And it is worth noting all the activities to try and places to discover because whilst there are no long stretches of grass to laze about on at Val d'Aleth, it is a perfect base to embark on daily adventures.

Most of the surrounding towns and villages have feudal or fascinating histories. Limoux, for instance, is a town known for its fizzy Blanquette wine, which is reputed to be the original secret recipe from which champagne was made. If ever you needed an excuse to drink in an atmosphere, this must be it. Production of this bubbly (which is less gassy than Cava) continues apace at vineyards such as Domaine de Fourn where you can have a tour and then buy a few bottles for consumption back at base. After a glass or two or three, you may well find yourself discussing whether Limoux should open a swimming pool and fill it with their local fizz. Now, that would be truly decadent.

THE UPSIDE: Lazy, shady riverside spot; easy to get to for a quick break.

THE DOWNSIDE: A few days won't give you enough time to do the environs justice but a longer stay might leave the tent campers hankering for more space.

THE DAMAGE: Pitches start at €14 per night for a tent and 2 people with a car or camper van. There are 2 caravans for hire from €115 for a 3-day stay. Three B&B rooms in their stunning town house, each with its own bathroom, cost a very reasonable €47 for 2 (in one room).

THE FACILITIES: You'll find six centrally heated showers and toilets, a dishwashing area, a washing machine and tumble dryer. There's also a play area, bike hire and BBQ. Off site a mini-stadium offers volleyball and basketball, and there are various walking trails.

FOOD AND DRINK: Domaine de Fourn (11300 Pieusse; 00 33 4 68 31 15 03; www.robert-blanquette.com) offers tours to explain the production of their alcopop and you can buy a few bottles. If you prefer your drink *sans alcool*, you can stock up on the renowned bottled Alet mineral water in the village.

FAMILY FUN: A mile (1.6 km) away is one of France's celebrated tree-walking adventure parks. Harnessed challenges suit all ages at Accro' Parc (Le Moulin, 11580 Alet-les-Bains; 00 33 4 68 69 94 86) but you may not want to look down.

TREAT YOURSELF: To a revitalising plunge into the curing waters of Les Thermes d'Alet-les-Bains (00 33 4 68 69 90 27).

GETTING THERE: From Carcassonne it's just one road, on the D118 past Limoux. Follow the turning left over the stone bridge and the campsite is signposted from there.

PUBLIC TRANSPORT: Fly with Ryanair to Carcassonne or Perpignan. Major carriers also fly to Toulouse. You can take an SNCF train to Limoux. Buses go from Limoux and Carcassonne to Alet-les-Bains.

OPEN: All year (only mobile homes in the winter).

IF IT'S FULL: Follow the D118 past Quillon to Axat for Camping La Crémade, a campsite set amongst forest pine trees (11140 Aude; 00 33 4 68 20 50 64; www.lacremade.com).

Le Val d'Aleth, 11580 Alet-les-Bains	t	00 33 4 68 69 90 40	w	www.valdaleth.com

mas de la fargassa

An organic fruit farm that lives off its land – selling plums, apples, strawberries, gooseberries, raspberries, pears and 120 kilos of organic bread each week – needs some assistance, and the Dutch–English proprietors get it by offering work placements to young travellers. In exchange for free accommodation and food, the land is cultivated, the donkeys walked, brushed and fed, the bread kneaded every Friday (ready to sell at the wonderful Céret market on the Saturday) and the fires are lit at night.

Watching workers from all over the world busying themselves and relaxing so well together lends a really cool, traveller vibe to this location. Actually, the location is cool enough without them, and turns over as a family-friendly business in the height of summer. But anyone who's trekked to far-fetched lands will be impressed with the journey to get here. Don't even think of turning back along the windy 5½ mile (9 km) path that cuts through the mountains: once you've started, there's nowhere to turn around. Some people rate the view of the Gorges du Mondony as their holiday highlight, others will always regret having looked down. On a positive note, the smaller the vehicle, the less your vertigo-induced fear (mobile homes are a definite no-go).

It took Jerone and Madhu two years of travelling down never-ending roads to find their dream home. One day 11 years ago, they caught a glimpse of chimney smoke rising through a clearing in the trees. The owner of that particular home wasn't selling, but next door they spotted an isolated, dilapidated forge that had been uninhabited since the '30s. They snapped it up along with the surrounding 600 acres then set to work transforming rubbles of stone into fully functional, modern accommodation. Nowadays, they hire out a *gîte*, a chalet and a pigsty, which in total sleep 18 people.

Madhu and Jerone launched the camping bow in their arrow some seven years ago with their Dutch designed De Waard Albatros tents. Six equipped tents named after the trees they're next to (holly, plum etc.), sit by the stream or on a raised level overlooking the garden; plus, there's space for people to put up their own canvas. They built a covered eating area where 50 people have been known to crowd around dining tables for the mostly vegetarian evening meals. You can also swim in the river – making dams is apparently the holidaying proclivity of older Dutchmen – else just sit back and cook marshmallows over the fire.

It feels quite exciting to be so near to Spain in dense woodland. Whenever you fancy a change of national scenery, just hike over the border; there are two-hour and five-hour organised walks available. If you came in your own 4x4 you'll be able to make it over rocky terrain by car, maybe passing a few wild boars on the way. Madhu arranges regular group outings where you can hike to a Spanish restaurant for lunch, after which cars will bring you back. These trips are usually snapped up as it's good to stretch your legs without the worry of getting lost.

Lately, Madhu has been overseeing the construction of a second pigsty (perhaps better described as a two-person, one room studio). Whilst Jerone's been working on a tree house development overlooking the Spanish border. The couple have come a long way from Amsterdam where they previously ran a successful tea shop. It's a long way from anywhere, in fact. Their amazing, combined feat borne of patience, hard labour and assiduous planting enables them to sustain a living in this remote, unusual borderline setting. Hats off to them for living the (self-sufficient) dream.

THE UPSIDE: Organic living and river swimming.

THE DOWNSIDE: The narrow mountain road has a precipitous drop; it's not for the faint-hearted. Nor is it for those who like nipping out to the shops.

THE DAMAGE: Six equipped tents are €450 per week. The chalet (sleeps 5–6) is €550 per week. Two apartments (sleep 2 or 9) are €350/1025 per week. Campers with their own tent are charged €8 per person per night (there's no camping, though, in July and August).

THE FACILITIES: The shop sells campsite basics (bread, milk, coffee, alcohol). There's a washing machine, Internet (although, the line is often down), hot showers, kids' play area and a shared BBQ. No pets are allowed but they have their own cat, dog, chickens, donkeys and ponies.

FOOD AND DRINK: Home-baked bread, jams, chutney and organic vegetables and fruits are at your fingertips.

FAMILY FUN: Madhu offers regular donkey guided rides on a first-come first-served basis.

TREAT YOURSELF: To a traditional Catalan festival, where everyone parades in costume and kicks up their heels with a song and dance. Various local events take place over the summer.

GETTING THERE: Fly to Perpignan or Gerona, then hire a car or take a bus to Amélie-les-Bains. The road is in the eastern Pyrénées mountains, 20 minutes from Amélie-les-Bains by car, 50 minutes from Collioure. Heading south on the D115, after Amèlie-les-Bains, take the first left signposted to Gorges du Mondon, passing Mas Pagris village along a long dirt track (with a precipitous drop!). On its descent, there's a right turn into the driveway.

PUBLIC TRANSPORT: You can get a bus from Perpignan to Amélie-les-Bains. It's a two-hour walk from there or they may be able to pick you up.

OPEN: Apr–mid-Oct; other accommodation open all year round. May is a great time to see Céret's cherry blossom in full bloom.

IF IT'S FULL: There's not a lot in the area but back in Collioure is the *Cool Camping* seaside resort of Les Criques des Porteils (see p200).

Mas de la Fargassa, Montalba, 66110 Amélie-les-Bains	t	00 33 4 68 39 01 15	w	www.fargassa.com

les criques de porteils

Sun, sea, sand and sangria have long been the stereotypical staple holiday requirements of the British abroad. But, sun, sea, sand and sangria *en France*? Now, that's a more unusual combination...

Back in 1659 before the border separating Spain from France was drawn, Perpignan and the areas further south into northern Spain were collectively called Catalonia. It's a region that still exists in northeast Spain, but North Catalonia has long since evolved into the French-owned Roussillon. Families who found their villages suddenly divided by the French–Spanish frontier continued co-existing, farming and trading as before; and, proud of their heritage, their descendants in Roussillon, about a quarter of the current population, still speak the dialect of their ancestors' and a strong Catalan spirit reverberates.

Les Criques de Porteils lies 15 miles (25 km) south of Perpignan, just outside Collioure. The university town of Perpignan may be widely known, but Collioure is the more beautiful of the two. It's not just the sunny climate that exudes a Spanish feel there; the buildings are painted ochre, strains of flamenco music can be heard, street signs are in Catalan and, living up to its moniker as the 'city of painters', extra colour abounds from over 30 art galleries.

It's a good thing you can walk down to Collioure from the campsite in 30 minutes as parking there is nigh impossible, even in low season. The town overflows with fish restaurants and anchovies are a local speciality. That said, the campsite is opening its own sea-view fish restaurant in summer 2008, so there may be less of a reason for anyone to ever leave...

The turning off the D114 coastal road to the campsite is uninspiring at first. But once you've passed the mediocre-looking Hôtel du Golfe, you'll arrive at this hidden oasis. A spread of green trees seems to keep the lid on this semi-secret spot, whilst its seaward edge is marked handsomely by an undulating old stone wall built on the top of picturesque, squat cliffs. Below, a generally calm, flat tide sweeps back and forth across the Mediterranean, lapping gently at the three pebble beaches. A truly idyllic spot.

Five camping areas offer separate spaces for tents and statics. The first is at the entrance to the site, where you'll need to hurry past the 20 mobile units packed together. Beyond this anomaly, the sea-facing pitches are the most fantastically scenic, with stepped rows etched into the hill to ensure everyone can benefit from the view. Also on the campsite's coastal edge are eight pastel-green 'Bengali' tents – five-berth canvas bungalows, available for hire. They're basic, functional and totally tardis-like, with a covered decked terrace outside the front. At the other end of the site are two more sheltered camping areas, one that overlooks the foothills of the Albères and another where you'll glimpse the azure, blue waters glistening through the trees.

Les Criques has been a working campsite since 1965. New owners took over in 2006 and have already modernised bright children- and baby-changing rooms and have added a clothes shop. Plenty of assistance is on hand in the reception to help arrange anything – wine tasting, bowling, playing a game of golf, visiting one of the many adventure parks or day-tripping to Spain (Barcelona, a true Catalan city, is only a two-hour drive away).

But if that all seems like too much effort, spend all day on the beach and, at night, pour your own sangria into a plastic cup and raise a toast to your fellow campers, before letting the ocean lull you into a peaceful slumber.

THE UPSIDE: Three private beaches are solely for the campers' own use.

THE DOWNSIDE: Many pitches are on or near sand, which can get everywhere. Don't even think of arriving without a booking.

THE DAMAGE: Prices range between €19 and €32 for a tent and 2 people per night. Upgrading to an equipped Bengali tent costs €169–619 per week, depending on the season. If you turn up without booking and there's space they'll let you stay for up to three nights.

THE FACILITIES: It's a huge site with 250 tent pitches, 20 mobile homes (sleep 6) and eight Bengali tents (sleep 5). There are three shower blocks, a launderette, recycling bins, Internet, a heated swimming pool, tennis, *boules*, restaurant/bar/takeaway, but no BBQs.

FOOD AND DRINK: Catalan cooking abounds. The staff at the campsite rate the arty Hôtel Les Templiers (00 33 4 68 98 3110; www.hotel-templiers.com) so much they booked it for their end-of-season party.

FAMILY FUN: Visit the Musée d'Art Moderne (Villa Pams, Route de Port Vendres, 66190 Collioure; 00 33 4 68 82 10 19) for 20th-century and contemporary art (open daily).

TREAT YOURSELF: To some deep-sea diving. English-speaking instructors are based at the happening port of Argelès-sur-Mer. Expect to pay about €34 for a 20-minute taster session, up to €520 for a ten-dive block of lessons (00 33 4 68 95 89 49; www.divemania.nl).

GETTING THERE: From the airport at Perpignan, take the A9 turning off at exit 43 at Le Boulou. Follow signs to Argelès-sur-Mer then you should follow the D914 towards Collioure. Turn off at exit 13 and after 300 metres on your right is Hôtel du Golfe. Follow the road and signposts for the site.

PUBLIC TRANSPORT: Take the train from Perpignan to Collioure, the campsite is just over a mile (2 km) away.

OPEN: Apr–Sept.

IF IT'S FULL: The owners also run Camping Mar Estang in nearby Canet (Route de Saint-Cyprien, 66140 Canet-en-Roussillon; 00 33 4 68 80 35 53; www.marestang.com), although it's more commercial: it has disco nights, yoga lessons and even a visiting weekly market.

Camping Les Criques de Porteils, Corniche de Collioure, 66700 Argelès-sur-Mer

t 00 33 4 68 80 35 53 w www.lescriques.com

MADRID 606
AMSTERDAM
1094
19 CANET
1032 LONDRES
NEW YORK 6480
708 PARIS
1354 BERLIN

indigo rieumontagné

More Huttopian loveliness from these eco-warriors and it's their sunniest one at that (well, the furthest one south, even the team at *Cool Camping* can't guarantee the weather). In true Huttopia style, the building materials blend with the environment. Anything that's not made of stone or wood has been painted in environmentally friendly shades for an idyllic juxtaposition between mankind and the mountains.

The campsite juts into Lac du Laouzas in the Parc Régional du Haut Languedoc and at its tip, rows of shading trees give way to a long sandy beach. A beach, in the mountains? It's an unlikely but fantastic combination. The almighty lake spans some 750 acres with a water temperature that hits 22°C highs during the summer. This is an ideal spot to try your hand at fly-fishing; waiting for your hook are various perch, bass, rainbow trout and carp as well as white-footed crayfish.

Organised mountain trips offering views of the Mediterranean, the Pyrénées and many of France's southerly regions are a must. The day's hike to Caroux, to follow the wild Hérault goats (who themselves are following the sun) in their natural habitat is an incredible sight.

Camping Indigo attracts families on their fortnight- to month-long summer holidays, so if you're after a more exclusive travel experience you might find the domestic vibe's not for you. But otherwise, if you're a fan of mountains and luscious still waters you'll be dialling those digits already.

THE UPSIDE: Lakeside camping from our favourite French campsite chain.

THE DOWNSIDE: You can find tranquillity here but if you're seeking isolation then look elsewhere.

THE DAMAGE: Any of the 170 pitches cost between €13 and €19 for a tent and 2 people; plus there's a booking fee. Weekly rates for mobile homes start at €190, chalets from €290.

THE FACILITIES: Five regularly cleaned shower/toilet blocks are spread out on a site that also has a reception, a café-restaurant and a communal BBQ. Fridges and security deposits are available. If you're a sports fan, you can pick between volleyball, *boules*, basketball and aqua gym classes. Others might like to play their video and board games.

FOOD AND DRINK: Pink garlic bulbs grow in the chalky soil at Lautrec, the other side of Castres. Their therapeutic benefits can be enjoyed raw, roasted whole on your campfire or chopped up into all kinds of dishes. Closer to camp, the Lacaune region specialises in dried salted meats, so fill up on hams, sausages, *melsat* (made with meat, bread and eggs), black puddings and the like.

FAMILY FUN: La Salvetat-sur-Agoût has over 185 miles (300 km) of mountain bike trails for all levels. Ask at the reception about bike hire.

TREAT YOURSELF: To a breathtaking leap across a chasm. Cap'Découverte (81450 Le Garric; 00 33 8 25 08 12 34; www.capdecouverte.com) boasts Europe's longest 'zip-line' where you harness yourself (and up to two others) onto a cable then fly off.

GETTING THERE: From Toulouse it's an easy drive to Castres, then take the D622 to Nages and you can't miss it.

OPEN: Mid-June–mid-Sept.

IF IT'S FULL: Try Domaine Lacanal (81320 Nages; 00 33 5 63 37 25 10; www.lacanal.com), also in Nages. As well as hiring tent pitches, they also have a fully equipped tent for four and a few B&B rooms.

Camping Indigo Rieumontagné, Lac du Laouzas, 81320 Nages

t	00 33 5 63 37 24 71	w	www.camping-indigo.com

les chalets du tarn

Professional rally drivers might slide round the corners of these winding country roads with ease but speed here is not to be recommended, however much fun it might be. Stick to second gear all the way down this tricky mountain descent and, sunglasses at the ready: prepare to be stunned. Cut into a gorge at Pont de Lincou where the River Tarn idles by is Les Chalets du Tarn, the best-kept local camping secret.

Manoeuvring around tight bends gives your arms a jolly good work out, until you're abruptly halted by the sheer yet simple magnificence of your surroundings. Your rally-driving mind may feel like yanking on the handbrake at the riverside crossroads, to soak in the village and the woods – but you'll have plenty of time to explore this diminutive hamlet later. For now, turn right and pass Château de Lincou into Les Chalets du Tarn. Passing 15 wooden chalets, you arrive at the start of 21 pitches scattered amongst a thicket of forest trees.

The site is run by a couple that wanted to escape Paris and live 'the good life' in the countryside. Travelling through the area one year they spotted a 'closed' sign and asked the owner if he wanted to sell. He said yes, and, bingo, here they are fulfilling tasks such as renting canoes and kneading pizza dough for the two daily meals they serve.

What the village of Pont du Lincou lacks in size it makes up for with charisma and in ambience. You'll feel like you're in another world. But, shh, don't go telling everyone.

THE UPSIDE: Tranquil camping in a hidden valley.

THE DOWNSIDE: There isn't one that we've seen. You'll have to come back to us on this one.

THE DAMAGE: Tent and 2 people cost €10–15 per night. Chalets €270–550 per week.

THE FACILITIES: The on-site terraced bar offers evening meals. A *plat du jour* costs €8 or go all out for a full three-course spread for a budget-friendly €11.50. It's 10 minutes by car to Requista where there's a supermarket and tourist office.

FOOD AND DRINK: Buy a crusty *baguette* and some blue, crumbly Roquefort cheese, the gastronomic forté of the Aveyron region. The campsite's valley lies between Millau and Albi, so you're also right next to the fabulous Château de Lincou restaurant-bar (00 33 5 65 78 50 41).

FAMILY FUN: Throughout the summer, villages take it in turns to host *fêtes*. Pont du Lincou usually takes the baton the first weekend in August.

TREAT YOURSELF: To a picnic on the beaches of the 'French Lake District'. The massive Lac de Pareloup at Lévézou is an hour's drive away.

GETTING THERE: The A68 gets you from Toulouse to Albi pretty swiftly. From there hop onto the D903 to Requista, passing the church and a left turn on the D902 to the River Tarn. It's a long drive from Clermont-Ferrand (exit Millau) on the A75, then east on the D908 then north on the D902. Follow the D2088 from Rodez onto the D902, also south, all the way to the river.

PUBLIC TRANSPORT: Ryanair will fly to Rodez from London Stansted from the end of April 2008, otherwise Toulouse is the nearest main airport. SNCF trains run to Rodez. There is a bus service between Requista and Rodez.

OPEN: Mid-June–mid-Sept; chalets available from late-March.

IF IT'S FULL: Follow the River Tarn and cross over at Millau and into the lovely village of Boyne where there's the Moulin de la Galinière site (00 33 5 65 62 65 60; www.moulindelagaliniere.com).

Les Chalets du Tarn, Pont du Lincou, Requista, 12170 Tarn-et-Garonne

t 00 33 5 65 72 34 84 | w www.leschaletsdutarn.com

OIGNONS DOUX
Fruits
ACCUEIL
RESTAURANT
BOUTIQUE
La CORCONNE
GITES
CHALETS

la corconne

Eric Colomb lives right at the back of the dense woods in a building that, camouflaged by branches, looks suspiciously like an oversized tree house. Having grown up here, he took over the management of his father's campsite 14 years ago. Life was very different during his childhood in Cévennes. Before a motorway was built linking Paris to the south and, more recently, before Norman Foster's Millau Viaduct speeded up the passage across the Massif Central mountainous range, residents lived in relative isolation. Despite any pressures to move with the times, Eric's philosophy is to eschew modern lifestyle trends in favour of tried-and-tested simplicity.

You reach La Corconne off a picturesque route linking Millau with Nîmes. There are no high rises with satellite dishes. No burger chains. No-one sporting the latest hairdressing fashions. Just narrow roads weaving their way around stunning vistas, broken only by wafts of chimney smoke rising from hillside shacks. Just south of Valleragué is a tiny bridge (too small for caravans) leading into thick woods. Here, six *gîtes* have been carved into the rugged forest to blend with nature's colours and 33 pitches are spread amongst the trees and a neighbouring field. In keeping with the arboreal harmony, Eric used the felled green oaks and chestnuts to help build a large chalet, which they also rent out, and a dining hut that, reached by a footbridge, wouldn't look out of place on a Thai beach.

Cévennes became a national park in 1970 in order to protect and preserve its myriad valleys, ravines and gullies. All this dense woodland attracts a menagerie of friendly creatures to the campsite, so don't be surprised to see lizards, butterflies, squirrels and rabbits shuffling amongst the leaves. One holidaying botanist recently counted 17 different types of plants and shrubbery from the comfort of her deckchair. And, what's more, all these nesting opportunities intensify the most wondrous birdsong at dawn.

Eric considers La Corconne to be a perfect choice, particularly because children are happy to splish and splosh about in the water of the River Hérault all day long, leaving parents to enjoy quality down time. Whenever you fancy an outing, there are plenty of walks nearby but you'll need a car to explore the surrounding area. In the evening, the gentle itinerary continues: one live music performance is the sole weekly entertainment on site. Instead, campers 'connect' as a family and do very little except loll around their tent before devouring Eric and Maria's candlelit suppers.

Energetic ramblers might like to climb nearby Mont Aigoual for a stunning view that sweeps from the Alps along the coast to the Pyrénées. It's an eight-hour expedition there and back, so less-committed walkers should enquire about shorter hikes. Also top of the list should be a trip to the tourist-driven River Tarn, to swim in its famous canyons, before continuing on to Millau to shop among its cobbled alleyways.

Back in the sixties, this region's back-to-basics lifestyle attracted a mini-wave of hippies, some of whom camped out at La Corconne. Although they've since moved on to more conservative pastures, their children and grandchildren keep coming back year after year after year. If Eric's seen any change since the decade of peace and love it's that, although people still like camping in simple tents, they now bring them in fancier, sometimes very expensive, cars.

You're in deep, deep countryside here so Eric welcomes those who respect the primitive nature of the environment. Whilst you won't exactly be rubbing two sticks together (fires are not permitted in these woods) you might well find yourself hunter-gathering. Well, for your children at least.

THE UPSIDE: Back-to-basics camping in the woods.

THE DOWNSIDE: It's totally, utterly dark at night. Bring a torch and/or gas light. (Eric did once put lights up but regulars complained they couldn't see the stars.)

THE DAMAGE: Two people with tent and a car is €11–13 per night. Six *gîtes* (sleeping 2) cost between €380 and €490 per week; the chalet (sleeps 7) is €190–280 per person per week.

THE FACILITIES: You can pre-order evening meals and the shop sells ice creams, cold drinks, beer and Fair Trade items, as well as the usual basics.

FOOD AND DRINK: Taste the raw, sweet tang of *oignons doux*, the local speciality of southern Cévennes. A jar of *confit d'oignons* relish on sale at a roadside kart outside the campsite goes brilliantly with breads and pâtés.

FAMILY FUN: Order wood-fired pizzas at the campsite or go to Pizzas Nonna in Valleraugue (quai André Chamson; 00 33 6 31 13 13 90) for equally tasty versions.

TREAT YOURSELF: To days of doing nothing, except swinging from the trees, reading and playing pooh sticks.

GETTING THERE: Driving from the south, turn off the D999 that connects Millau with Nîmes, onto the D986 towards Valleraugue. Before the village turn right at a small bridge. Blink and you'll miss it.

PUBLIC TRANSPORT: Fly to Marseille or Nîmes then take a bus that stops at Pont d'Hérault 2 miles (3 km) from the site.

OPEN: Apr–Oct; all year for huts and chalets.

IF IT'S FULL: Camping Cévennes-Provence (Corbès-Thoiras, 30140 Anduze; 00 33 4 66 61 73 10) for a similar if more modern concept of woodland riverside camping, where the Gardon de Mialet and Saint-Jean du Gard rivers join.

Camping La Corconne, Route Départemental 986, 30570 Valleraugue

t 00 33 4 67 82 46 82 w www.lacorconne.com

Cevennes
PRÉHISTORAMA
Musée des origines et de l'évolution de l'homme
A 300m
EXPOSITION GRATUITE
EVES ET RÊVES
Les Vénus préhistoriques
du 1er juillet au 30 novembre 2007
Venez visiter nos Jardins...
STOP
PROVENCE
FISCHER
BIERE D'ALSACE
OPEN

beau rivage

Marc Vincke calls his little part of the world 'paradise', and he's not wrong. Even finding the place is a breeze. No zigzagging along endless country lanes to get here, and with direct routes from various cities you can shop around for cheap flights. And shouldn't all roads to paradise be paved with gold? Well, if you come via Alès, you'll see people panning for the stuff.

There are 190 pitches, so in *Cool Camping* terms it's not an intimate paradise. But there's something calming about the landscape. Beau Rivage begins at Marc's home, which looks over flat meadows. On the far left, the land drops down to the river. Pitches are spaced amongst the trees, so even when full, the aura remains peaceful.

Aim for a spot at the bottom by the Cèze river. You're further away from the comings-and-goings of other campers and ideally positioned for quick refreshing dips. Swimming is the main attraction here.

Any adventurous escapades require a car; you can drive to the south coast in two hours or to the mountains of the Parc National des Cévennes in one. Alès, the nearest town, is full of pavement eateries for a decent pit-stop. There's a prehistoric museum (Musée de Préhistoire) nearby and if that sparks your imagination, check out the decorated caves at Chauvet Pont d'Arc, where people lived during the Stone Age. Men in loincloths? Gold? That sounds like some ladies kind of paradise, for sure.

THE UPSIDE: Green ambient pastures exude a quiet camping festival vibe.

THE DOWNSIDE: There's not much going on locally. But big cities and monumental sights of nature are only a drive away.

THE DAMAGE: Prices per night: adult €6, child €3, tent or caravan and car €5, more for electricity charges depending on ampage.

THE FACILITIES: There's a morning visit from a baker and a postman, a reception selling ice creams, cold drinks and camping gas, plus a shared washing machine, hot and cold showers, wi-fi and a shared BBQ.

FOOD AND DRINK: The Beau Rivage hot tip is the Asian restaurant L'Auberge d'Auzon at Allègre-Les Fumades (rue de l'Ancien Couvent, Auzon; 00 33 4 66 24 83 51).

FAMILY FUN: Time travel back to when man wore loincloths and hunted for supper with a spear at Le Musée de Préhistoire (avenue Léon-Jean Grégory, 66720 Tautavel; 00 33 4 68 29 07 76).

TREAT YOURSELF: To a spot of gold panning near the River Gardon d'Anzuze on the D6110 (00 33 4 66 83 67 35).

GETTING THERE: Off the D904 north of Alès take the D37 at Saint-Ambroix (so it's the right fork) and continue until you see signs on the left for the campsite.

PUBLIC TRANSPORT: You can fly to Nîmes, Montpellier or Valence and hire a car from there. Buses run from Montpellier up to three times a day to Saint-Ambroix.

OPEN: Apr–mid-Sept.

IF IT'S FULL: Camping-Caravaning Le Clos has 90 sizeable grassy pitches and a swimming pool (30500 Saint-Ambroix; 00 33 4 66 24 10 08; www.camping-le-clos.com).

Camping Beau Rivage, Le Moulinet, 30500 Saint-Ambroix

t 00 33 4 66 24 10 17 | w www.camping-beau-rivage.fr

VAUDE

le clapas

Le Clapas might sound like the kind of thing you'd do to a Ricky Martin track – but 'clapas' is actually an old Occitan name for a pile of stones – or a building made from a pile of stones. In the case of Camping Le Clapas, the stones come from a beach slap bang on the Ardèche river – the robust rivulet that forged the beautiful gorges found in this area and which gave the *département* its name.

A former municipal spot, Le Clapas was taken over sometime around 2005 and transformed into something a little more special. Trees were planted, small walls were built using the eponymous stones, which still line the river banks and the site's private beach. Plus, the facilities were tweaked and expanded to make the site more cosy, imaginative and comfortable.

You'll find the 75 decent-sized pitches beneath a swaying miscellany of acacias and pines, and many (though not all) offer views of the Ardèche. It's a family-friendly place, with *boules*, table tennis and volleyball on offer and regular group entertainments, such as BBQs, themed evenings and karaoke. The adults are catered for too, with a small but well-stocked on-site bar.

Thanks to the river, canoeing and kayaking are big draws here. And, there is something for everyone – gentle stretches for beginners, and drifters and feisty rapids for the adrenaline fiends. Le Clapas works in partnership with a local tour operator to arrange canoe and kayak tours for individuals, groups and families that leave directly from the site; these range from a leisurely 5-mile (8-km) paddle to a more strenuous 20-mile (32-km) trip.

If river-related shenanigans don't grab you, there are plenty of other diversions. The surroundings are nothing short of delightful. The most obvious – the Gorges de l'Ardèche – feature limestone cliffs that reach up to 300 m high; one of the most popular sights along the way is the natural 60 m stone arch known as the Pont d'Arc, which hogs much of the local publicity material. It happens to be a particularly pleasant hour's stroll from the site; take your swimmers as it also has a beach.

Amateur speleologists (that's cavers to you and me) and other interested parties might also want to visit Chauvet whilst there; this Paleolithic network of caves contains paintings and engravings estimated to be

between 17,000 and 20,000 years old. The site, up there with Lascaux and Cosquer, is a must-see for most people, though choose your viewing time carefully to avoid the crush of the coach-crowds.

The local region is studded with what are known as *villages de caractère* – timeless symbols of the area's rural heritage heavily marketed by the tourist board. Once you see them in the flesh, however, it's hard to refute their obvious wow factor.

Balazuc and Vogüé in particular are worth heading to. The former hangs off a steep hill and cliff-top and is surrounded by trees; the latter is a similarly stunning collection of stone houses huddled together beneath an imposing 17th-century *château*.

The site really comes into its own as a chilled retreat from the summer-time masses. With over 100,000 tourists descending on the area throughout July and August alone, it can be difficult not to feel a bit smug as you chill on a hammock or paddle in peace, while the 250+ pitch resorts across the river milk the masses with over-priced activities and tacky *discothèques*.

We have to say: it's much better to be doing Le Clapas; let the others do Ricky Martin.

THE UPSIDE: Right on the Ardèche river with its own private beach: killer.

THE DOWNSIDE: The area (though not the site) can be pretty crowded in summer.

THE DAMAGE: Tent and 2 people is €13–16.50, depending on the season. An extra adult costs €4–5.50 and a child (2–10 years) between €2 and €4.

THE FACILITIES: All the amenities you'll need are here, except a restaurant. There are two modern sanitary blocks with hot water plus washing machines, grocery store and snack bar – and everything is clean and functions well.

FOOD AND DRINK: Pizza and *frîtes* are served up on site throughout the summer, but for pukka Provençal food check out Le Vieux Vallon in Vallon Pont d'Arc (rue du Barry; 00 33 4 75 88 04 42). Great pâtés and potato dishes are served up in a charming old house. Vallon Pont d'Arc also has a regular market every Thursday and a food market every Sunday in high season.

FAMILY FUN: For via Ferrata (tree climbing), try Vert Tige (00 33 4 75 88 02 61; www.vert-tige-ardeche.com) in Vallon Pont d'Arc. Cave trips for kids over 10 can be arranged in Aven d'Orgnac (00 33 4 75 38 65 10; www.orgnac.com).

TREAT YOURSELF: To a stay in a castle. Head to Balazuc and discover how chic Moroccan tadelakt interiors go hand in hand with medieval fireplaces and Romanesque exteriors at the striking Château de Balazuc (00 33 4 75 88 52 67; www.chateaudebalazuc.com).

GETTING THERE: From Aix-en-Provence, take the A8 to Salon-de-Provence. Take the A7 towards Orange. Continue through Orange on the E15 and turn off towards Vallon Pont D'Arc. Follow the signs to Salavas and then keep a look out for signs to Le Clapas.

PUBLIC TRANSPORT: The closest you can get is Vallon Pont d'Arc, which is accessible by train or bus. From there, the site is a 25-minute walk or a taxi ride (about €13).

OPEN: Apr–late-Sept.

IF IT'S FULL: Most of the sites around the Ardèche river are coach-filled commercial resorts. Luckily there's a calmer option just along the river at Le Pequelet (00 33 4 75 88 04 49; www.lepequelet.com), also in Salavas. A leafy place with decent facilities and a private beach, it has a similar appeal to Le Clapas.

Camping Le Clapas, Salavas, 07150 Vallon Pont d'Arc	t	00 33 4 75 37 14 76	w	www.camping-le-clapas.com

les roulottes de saint-cerice

Situated 'twixt the gorges of the Ardèche and the Cévenoles mountains, Les Roulottes de Saint-Cerice is an idyllic secluded estate that is home to four vividly coloured *roulottes* (old-fashioned gypsy caravans), nestled amidst 12 or so acres of assorted swaying Mediterranean foliage.

The interiors of the *roulottes* are country-style – all light-wooden fittings and chequered reds and yellows, which create a suitably old-fashioned look. The beds are comfortable (there's room enough for up to four people comfortably – five at a push) and all the amenities you'd expect are there.

The owners have thoughtfully provided benches and plastic seats for outside relaxation, and if you find it hard to get going in the morning they can even make your breakfast for you (for a small charge). The grounds are gorgeously rural. Donkeys graze in fields, the smell of olive trees, thyme and rosemary wafts through the air and the vistas from the hillside are fabulous.

A 10-minute walk away is the medieval town of Vogüé; and just a little further on are the famed Ardèche gorges – a splendid wilderness area great for hiking and cycling. Water lovers are well catered for, too, since the Ardèche river is a top destination for canoe and kayak enthusiasts.

And the entire area is blessed with several of France's *plus beaux villages* – Vogüé amongst them – so, it's highly unlikely you're going to be stuck for interesting and cool stuff to do. Unless, of course, that's precisely the plan...

THE UPSIDE: Caravan-style camping in an idyllic setting.

THE DOWNSIDE: Off the beaten track; you need your own transport to get around.

THE DAMAGE: The *roulottes* cost €89–140 per night, €198–280 for a weekend and €534–890 for a week, depending on the season.

THE FACILITIES: The caravans have most facilities built-in but there's also a pool, tennis court and you can hire bicycles from the site.

FOOD AND DRINK: Down in Vogüé, the local *bistrot de pays* vends Provençal classics and Ardèche specialities like *caillettes* (meatballs). It's also worth trying some Ardèche wines, which tend to be excellent (whites and reds) and reasonably priced.

FAMILY FUN: The pool is open May to September. But it's only a 10-minute walk to the river so kayaking and canoeing are always an option.

TREAT YOURSELF: To some flying lessons in a glider or light aircraft. Ask at reception for details.

GETTING THERE: From Nice head towards Cagnes/Cannes/Aix-en-Provence. Get onto the A8 and merge onto the A7. Take exit 18-Montélimar-Sud toward Montélimar. Follow the signs to Vogüé, then signs to Les Roulottes de Saint-Cerice.

PUBLIC TRANSPORT: Buses run from most major towns to Vogüé, which leaves a 10-minute (uphill) walk to the site. Pick-ups are available on request.

OPEN: All year round.

IF IT'S FULL: Try the *Cool Camping* site Camping Le Clapas (see p214) – a lovely, leafy, friendly site right on the banks of the Ardèche river. Saint-Cerice also offers a farmhouse-style villa that can sleep up to 12 people (it comes with a private pool) and there are another two rooms inside the main family house.

Les Roulottes de Saint-Cerice, Saint-Cerice, 07200 Vogüé | t 00 33 4 75 37 08 66 | w www.saintcerice.com

Quechua

les oliviers

Chances are the area around Les Oliviers will have charmed the pants off you before you even arrive at the site. The drive there through the Provence countryside – think pretty villages, sun-kissed orchards and manicured vineyards – is simply stunning. The listed village of Eygalières continues the need for superlative descriptions as it tumbles down from a summit in the Alpilles hills. But this is just the warm-up act.

Even after such a memorable preamble, the campsite doesn't disappoint. *Au contraire.* This family-run place goes back three generations to 1963. Its 33 pitches (for tents and caravans), all tucked in amongst almond and olive trees, strike an immediate chord that reverberates throughout your stay.

There aren't an abundance of amenities. The basics are all included (electricity and water points, decent showers and bathrooms, a reception with information), but since the site is literally an olive toss away from the high street of Eygalières, everything you'll need (and more) is right on your doorstep.

Eygalières has are all kinds of shops and conveniences, from a baker's and a butcher's, to a grocery store and a chemist – there's even a post office should you need to finally send that postcard home that you've been clinging onto since Paris or Nice.

On the sightseeing front, the town offers several highlights, such as Chapelle Saint-Sixte (which dates from the 17th century), a local history museum with prehistoric relics (located inside Chapelle des Pénitents) and a small, pretty hermitage that lies just over half a mile (1 km) out of town.

You're spoilt for choice here in terms of outdoor activities. The village is right on the long-distance walking route GR6, and cyclists can hit the D24 from Eygalières and take a tour round some of the Alpilles landscapes (hire a bike from the site if you didn't bring yours). Don't be surprised if you see some famous types along the way. Actor and *bon vivant* Jean Claude Brialy (one of France's most respected cultural figures with over 180 films, a slew of theatre performances and numerous novels to his name) lived here until he passed away in 2007; and Alain Prost still calls Eygalières home, though you might have to have sharp eyesight to catch him whizzing past!

Further afield lie bigger treasures. Saint-Rémy-de-Provence – one of the 'must-sees' in Provence – lies only 6 miles (10 km) away. This historic village, built on one of the oldest archaeological sites in Europe, boasts beautifully restored old houses, lots of lovely fountains and an inordinate amount of elegant boutiques. The town is famous for many things, but mostly for its association with Vincent Van Gogh, who produced more than 150 paintings of the surrounding countryside during his time here.

Slightly further out in the Alpilles is the village of Les Baux-de-Provence, a magnificent, restored medieval village perched on a rock around fortified ruins. Perhaps due to its being labelled as 'one of the most beautiful villages in France' it's incredibly popular – perhaps overly much, given around 1.5 million tourists pass through its labyrinthine interior every year. There's no doubting the village's exquisite charm, nor its cultural value, but it's worth trying to get here early in the morning to avoid the masses.

An olive catapult away (just 400 metres if we're being pedantic) is a stable with horse riding (lessons and trekking are available) and if you're a tennis fiend, then grab your racket and balls and head for the tennis court down the road (ask at reception).

Oh, and in case you were wondering what happens to the eponymous olives – they're harvested around November time and taken to a local mill to make olive oil for the owners and their family. If you ask nicely, they might let you have some!

THE UPSIDE: Impossibly cute and impressively neat campsite, with peerless access to pretty Eygalières and the Provence countryside.

THE DOWNSIDE: There's a discernable lack of water (no rivers, lakes or pools) to cool off in.

THE DAMAGE: It's €12 per night for a pitch with 2 people. Additional adults cost €3 and children (3–8 years) €2.

THE FACILITIES: It's a small site and what it does have – hot water, electricity points, decent showers and washing-up sinks – is great.

FOOD AND DRINK: The local market days are Friday mornings (Eygalières) and Wednesday and Saturday mornings at Saint-Rémy-de-Provence. There's an *épicerie* on the high street and organic wine buffs can visit Domaine de Costebonne 2 miles (3 km) away at Cave du Mas Longchamp (Route de la Gare, Mollégès, 13940 Eygalières; 00 33 4 90 95 23 54). La Ferme d'Eygalières (Route d'Orgon, 13810 Eygalières; 00 33 4 90 90 62 14) offers a memorable set-price lunch.

FAMILY FUN: Horse riding lessons, courses and treks can be arranged at Eygalières Riding Centre (00 33 6 16 17 03 68; lesgrandesterres.free.fr). There is also a great zoo at La Barben (00 33 4 90 55 19 12; www.zoolabarben.com), about 25 miles (40 km) or 40 minutes by car away.

TREAT YOURSELF: To an 18th-century Provençal-style hotel experience at nearby Mas du Pastre (00 33 4 90 95 92 61; www.masdupastre.com). Or foodies can stroll around the corner to Chez Bru (00 33 4 90 90 60 34; www.chezbru.com) – a Michelin-starred restaurant that offers a wildly contemporary take on local dishes.

GETTING THERE: Eygalières is situated halfway between Saint-Rémy-de-Provence and Cavaillon. Take Exit 25 for Cavaillon from the A7 motorway on to the D99. Once in the village, follow the 'Camping' signposts.

PUBLIC TRANSPORT: Trains run to Cavaillon, 6 miles (10 km) from the site. Buses run both from Cavaillon (30 minutes away) and from Avignon (50 minutes away) a few days a week, and stop at the high street in Eygalières. From there it's 200 metres or so to the site.

OPEN: Apr–Nov.

IF IT'S FULL: Check out the charming alternative of Camping Le Pesquié (Route du Mas d'Aubergue, 13810 Eygalières; 00 33 4 90 95 99 50; www.camping-pesquie.com) 1½ miles (2.5 km) outside Eygalières – a small, farm-based campsite located in the countryside.

Les Oliviers, avenue Jean Jaurès, 13810 Eygalières	t	00 33 4 90 95 91 86	w	www.camping-les-oliviers.com

les matherons

Seventeen years ago, Les Matherons literally consisted of one house and two fields. There was no electricity, no water – and certainly nothing in the way of 'facilities'. The transformation from isolated wilderness to stunning rural campsite has taken a while, but if anyone ever needed further evidence that perseverance can make dreams come true, you'll find it here.

The dream in question belonged to Henk and Ada Knol, a Dutch couple looking to set up a campsite 'somewhere' in France. They knew the kind of spot they wanted, but it took them a remarkable 10 years before they found the place they now happily call home.

Though it could be (and is) regarded as off the beaten track, the campsite is in a deceptively good location. It's close enough to the motorway to make it just an hour and a half's drive from the sea and just an hour by car to the Alps and the Gorges du Verdon. Significant southern hubs like Aix-en-Provence and Marseille are also only an hour or two drive away.

Yet, Les Matherons (the name doesn't mean anything by the way – the owners just liked the way it sounded) remains something of a 'frontier campsite'. The closest town, Puimichel – a 20-minute walk along a small path – is home to just 250 souls; the next biggest town, Oraison (6 miles/10 km), only has 5000. There are 25 pitches, some of which require a bit of a hunt, and though cars are allowed on the campsite for arrival and for departure, they must be left in a dedicated parking spot outside the main site for the remainder.

The land spans over 130 acres, yet only 10 acres of the site is pragmatically used – the rest is a wonderful wilderness, left to grow organically with no attempts to 'tame' or 'landscape' it. Most of the pitches are located at the peripheries of two fields, each one about 15,000 square metres and are surrounded by oak trees (the owners planted all of the trees). But some of the more isolated spots, are accessible only with a bit of a hike.

Such dedication to a 'natural' camping experience is a big part of Les Matheron's appeal. The Knols are very upfront on their website, saying that certain types of camper might not enjoy the site. They point out there's no lighting (apart from in the sanitary block), no smooth-surfaced roads and that music and noisy activities are not welcome. 'People who are nervous of large grasshoppers or lizards will not be happy here,' they add – and they're not wrong.

There's plenty of natural space for adults and kids alike to romp around in, with none of the dangers of cars, rivers or lakes. And a couple of times a week there's food available on site (once a week it's vegetarian).

Though the site itself offers blissful respite from the outside world, there are diversions and distractions aplenty in the surrounding area. The local landscape is just as rugged, an undulating run of valleys, forests and fields, much of it uncultivated. During summer, lavender fills many of the surrounding fields, lending its distinctive and memorable hue to the already colourful Provençal scenery. Many of the walks are unmarked and some require strong shoes, though there are also plenty of opportunities on the roads for cyclists.

Even though Puimichel is small, it has an observatory and offers some great insights into local village life. Larger Oraison has more going on, with many activities, including fishing and swimming in the lakes (lifeguards, pedal-boats and windsurfing available) and easy access into the region's two main nature parks: the Luberon and the Verdon.

As for Ada and Henk, they've never been happier. Not only do they get to live their dream, they get to help other people experience it too.

THE UPSIDE: Wilderness camping for those who relish time alone with Mother Nature.
THE DOWNSIDE: It's not accessible by public transport.
THE DAMAGE: €7.50 per pitch plus €4 for adults and €3 for children.
THE FACILITIES: The large communal sanitary block is modern and has nice hot showers. There's a washing machine, a snack bar in reception sells basic snacks and sundries, and there's a pleasant playground area for kids.
FOOD AND DRINK: Puimichel's one-and-only restaurant Chez Jules (00 33 4 92 74 98 10) is run by the young and affable Émile and Christophe who posit a changing menu based on the availability of local products. Regional specialities can be found at the village's multi-service *épicerie* and at the markets at Oraison (Tuesday mornings) and Gréoux-les-Bains (25 miles/40 km) away (Thursdays).
FAMILY FUN: There are free public swimming pools in some of the nearby towns (ask at reception for details), and the astronomical observatory in Puimichel (00 33 6 37 43 00 42) may provoke a nascent interest in stargazing. There's also rafting two hours away, and you could drive to the coast for the day.
TREAT YOURSELF: To a relaxing massage or downtime in the spa, 18 miles (30 km) away in Dignes-les-Bains (Les Thermes des Digne, 04005 Dignes-les-Bains; 00 33 4 92 32 32 92; www.eurothermes.com).
GETTING THERE: From Grenoble, take the N75 or N85 (Route Napoléon) to Sisteron. At Sisteron take the N85 to Malijai. At the first roundabout after Malijai go to the right towards Les Mées. In Les Mées take the D4 to Oraison. Cross Oraison and follow the D12 towards Puimichel. Just over 1 mile (2 km) before Puimichel you will see the sign for Les Matherons.
OPEN: mid-Apr–Oct.
IF IT'S FULL: Camping L'Olivette about 12 miles (20 km) away in Les Pourcelles (04190 Les Mées; 00 33 4 92 34 18 97) is a small, sweet campsite with 25 pitches and friendly owners.

Camping Les Matherons, 04700 Puimichel	t	00 33 4 92 79 60 10	w	www.campinglesmatherons.com

Outwell

camping des gorges du verdon

'When the weather is fine you know it's the time for messin' about on the river. If you take my advice there's nothing so nice as messin' about on the river.' You may find these lyrics – or ones like them – ricocheting around your head on more than one occasion as you settle into this riverside spot in the Gorges du Verdon – France's greatest natural attraction and the world's second largest gorge.

To save you the time with your map, piece of string and a calculator – the Gorges du Verdon are about 12 miles (20 km) long and 300 metres deep. They were formed by the unstoppable force of water known as the River Verdon – so-called because of its distinctively emerald hue.

Camping des Gorges du Verdon is slap bang on the river, in the very heart of the Parc Naturel Régional du Verdon. Covering some 17 acres and resting at a very pleasant altitude of 660 metres, it's a wonderfully leafy place that's dotted with pinewoods and has all the hallmarks of a well-loved family-run spot. In fact, the site celebrated its 50th anniversary in 2008 and has been in the same family for all that time – these guys are nothing if not experienced!

The 100 pitches are flat and allow easy access for vehicles; they're sizeable and come with plenty of natural shade from the trees. There are chalets on site, but they're in a separate area from the camping pitches.

Being right on a river in a lovely large gorge obviously creates a wealth of recreational options. Without leaving the not-so-small confines of the site, you can relax on the beaches, try your hand at a spot of fly fishing or organise rafting, canyoning, canoeing, spring tide swimming or aquatic walks. And if you're not a big river swimmer (the temperatures can get cool, especially out of season) then don't fret as the campsite offers an alternative freshen-up in the shape of a heated, outdoor swimming pool, which in July and August has its own certified lifeguard.

Other on-site activities include bowling, *boules* and volleyball, as well as a library and communal room with TV and video. Bird lovers can also enquire about the bird-watching tours, arranged through the local vulture association. Walking trips can be organised free of charge from the site, and the gorge's limestone is a popular choice with rock climbers, too – there are reckoned to be anything up to 1500 routes around, ranging from 20 metres to over 400 metres.

If you're camping with kids then the site has some great treats in store. Not only are there regular *animations* (clowns, magicians and sometimes music, though all in French), there are also music evenings, on-site recreational activities and games in the pool. Mum can have a rest from cooking as there's a decent bar/restaurant that serves up pizzas, ice creams and take-away meals. And if Dad wants to set up the BBQ, he can find fresh regional produce at the grocery store, along with other camping essentials like stoves and sun cream.

Just along the road is the charming medieval town of Castellane. It's instantly recognisable by the gigantic rock that juts dramatically skywards from the valley. Aside from the 18th-century stone chapel (Chapelle Nôtre-Dame-du-Rock) that sits atop, Castellane doesn't have any tourist sites as such, but it's a perfectly charming place to enjoy a stroll and a *café au lait*, and the best place to organise activities.

The regional park itself spans almost 500,000 acres and includes 43 towns within its reach, so if you tire of lazing by the river there's plenty to keep you occupied in the outlying regions.

The French Riviera is just an hour and a half away by car, but chances are you're not going to want to leave what amounts to one of Europe's largest natural playgrounds in any kind of hurry.

THE UPSIDE: A family-run, family-friendly riverside campsite slap bang in the middle of a regional park.

THE DOWNSIDE: Those seeking a quieter, off-the-beaten track site might prefer elsewhere.

THE DAMAGE: For 2 people with a tent, caravan or car a pitch is between €12 and €14, depending on the season. An additional person is €4–5.50 euros and a child (under 4) is €1.20–2.

THE FACILITIES: A decent spread of facilities – including a shop, pizza hut, Internet, ice cream shop, restaurant and pool – makes the site suitable for longer-term stays.

FOOD AND DRINK: Castellane has a market on Sundays and Wednesdays where you can find lots of local produce. For great French pancakes and fantastic views, try Le Mur d'Abeilles in the heart of the village of Rougon (00 33 4 92 83 76 33).

FAMILY FUN: A 90-minute family rafting trip for children from 6 years old (with parents) can be organised with Base Sport & Nature (00 33 4 93 05 41 18; www.basesportnature.com). And if you need a change of watery scene, then Castellane also has a public swimming pool.

TREAT YOURSELF: To a bungee jump from nearby Pont de l'Arnby (ask at reception for details) and take in the scenery – upside down.

GETTING THERE: From Nice, take the A8 *autoroute* west (direction Aix-en-Provence) and exit at Cannes. From the Cannes exit roundabout, follow the signs for Grasse, taking the limited-access road. From Grasse, take the N85 Route Napoléon to Castellane, and then follow the signs for Camping des Gorges du Verdon.

OPEN: May–mid-Sept.

IF IT'S FULL: The *Cool Camping* site of Domaine Chasteuil-Provence (see p234) has a similar set-up near the Verdon river, and is also family run.

Camping des Gorges du Verdon, Clos d'Aremus, Chasteuil, 04120 Castellane

t 00 33 4 92 83 63 54 w www.camping-gorgesduverdon.com

VAUDE

domaine chasteuil-provence

Way back in 1959, a family from Holland opened a campsite on the banks of the Verdon river at the mouth of the splendid Gorges du Verdon. Today, Domaine Chasteuil-Provence is still run by their descendants, who take great care to create a welcoming place for adults and kids alike.

The campsite itself is massive, spanning 500 or so acres; but the pitches (which at an average of 100 sq. m certainly verge on the generous side) sit handily on the nearly 20-acre patch beside the sparkling Verdon. The pitches are shaded naturally by an assortment of trees and, though the site is fairly large, the gentle whisper of leaves combined with the soft whoosh of the river perfectly illustrates the fact that the emphasis here is on the natural, not the commercial.

The facilities are extensive without being obtrusive with a well-organised reception, a reasonable restaurant, a handy shop, plus well-maintained toilet and shower blocks.

Being riverside, a host of aquatic activities naturally present themselves: canoeing and kayaking along the Verdon is a great way of experiencing the scale of the gorges. The owners have been working with a rafting partner for years and can easily arrange individual and family excursions.

If you don't fancy the river, but still want some water-based fun – simply sashay across to the heated pool. Walkers and climbers will be spoiled for choice, too, thanks to the abundance of hiking trails and climbing walls in the nearby area.

History – nay, prehistory – buffs will definitely want to check out Musée de Préhistoire des Gorges du Verdon (00 33 4 92 74 09 59; www.museeprehistoire.com), where you can discover how primitive peoples lived in the area. Examine the 400,000-year-old artefacts unearthed at the Grotte de la Baume Bonne (at the village of Quinson, a few miles west of Lac de Sainte-Croix) and then step back in time and wander around the fascinating Village Préhistorique. Plus, the museum organises regular events and activities for all ages.

The almond-shaped building in itself is a must-see, having been designed by celebrated British architect Norman Foster, who also created the impressive but delicate-looking viaduct at Millau.

RILLETTES
OU
TERRINE
AU FOIE GRAS
5.00€ pièce
16.00€
LA MAISON
J.M. BAILLES
Aux cèpes
Rosette entière
A la coupe

The Parc Naturel Régional du Verdon envelops an area of almost 200,000 hectares, and there are plenty of opportunities to explore this natural wonderland.

The cute cliff-top village of Castellane – about 2½ miles (4 km) away – is the place to get info and organise trips, though much can be arranged directly through the helpful people at reception.

If you have a car, a great scenic drive leaves Castellane and follows the D952 along the north rim of the canyon for 20 or so miles (30 km), taking in the Point Sublime – a popular spot with spectacular views along the canyon's narrow, deep cleft. A full drive around the whole 60-mile (100-km) rim takes an entire day with a few stops.

THE UPSIDE: Riverside spot with heated pool and the Verdon gorges a pebble-skim away.

THE DOWNSIDE: Whilst it's perfect for families, those looking for a quiet site might want to try elsewhere.

THE DAMAGE: Two people and a tent costs €11.90–22.80, depending on the season. Additional adults are charged at €3.50–5, and €1.80–2.60 for children (under 6).

THE FACILITIES: The facilities are very family-friendly, and include a heated pool, restaurant, playground and a well-stocked convenience store.

FOOD AND DRINK: There are pizzas, salads and such available on site. The rather sweet eaterie Auberge de Teillon (00 33 4 92 83 60 88; www.auberge-teillon.com), a family-run place on Route de Grasse in Le Garde, near Castellane, makes lovely meals like *le risotto aux morilles et St-Jacques* (morel and scallop risotto). Set *menus* start at €22.

FAMILY FUN: Throughout the summer the site organises entertainment twice a day for kids and can arrange extra family-style canoeing and walking trips. With so much land at your disposal, hide-and-seek is always an option!

TREAT YOURSELF: To a relaxing horse ride around the gorges and lakes. Ask at reception for details.

GETTING THERE: From Nice, take the A8 west (direction Aix-en-Provence) and exit at Cannes. From the Cannes-exit roundabout, follow the signs for Grasse, taking the limited-access road. From Grasse, take the N85 Route Napoléon to Castellane, and follow the signs for the campsite.

PUBLIC TRANSPORT: Regular buses from Nice to Grenoble stop at Castellane, and local bus services run from Castellane past the campsite twice a day.

OPEN: May–mid-Sept.

IF IT'S FULL: There's another *Cool Camping* site a few miles away – Gorges du Loup (see p240) is a similarly well-located and well-run spot.

Domaine Chasteuil-Provence, Route des Gorges du Verdon, 04120 Castellane

t	00 33 4 92 83 61 21	w	www.chasteuil-provence.com

2 km

les gorges du loup

Rumour has it that the main road that winds through the lovely Gorges du Loup was built by workers paid by the Cycling Club of France. True or not, the area is certainly a favoured cycling route today, and being just 35 minutes (by car) from the French Riviera, it remains one of the region's most popular all-round natural attractions.

Les Gorges du Loup is located close to Le Bar-sur-Loup, a *petit* medieval village with lots of lovely old houses clustered around a central 13th-century *château*. Perched on a rocky spur between Grasse and Vence, the village offers panoramic views of the Loup Valley. The site itself, a mile or so away, has 70 pitches (plus a few chalets and mobile homes) set on attractive terraced slopes where roses and lavender were once grown to make perfume. Though the pitches are fairly small, the site has an organic intimacy that's perfectly suited to the region.

To wear out the kids there's a decent-sized pool with a diving board and slide, and if you fancy a night off from cooking there's a restaurant and bar. It's in a prime location for all kinds of activities, from hang-gliding and climbing to cycling and hiking.

Plus there are lots of other pretty outposts to explore, such as Tourrettes-sur-Loup (see p243) and the *plus beaux* village of Gourdon (as seen in Hitchcock's *To Catch a Thief*). And don't worry – you don't have to be a cyclist to see them all. A car will do just fine.

THE UPSIDE: Verdant and natural site with fantastic access to the Gorges du Loup.

THE DOWNSIDE: Very family-friendly, so if you prefer a quiet life then choose another site.

THE DAMAGE: Two people with a tent/car is €20–24.20 (depending on the size of the pitch/tent). Additional people are charged at €4.20 (adults) and €3.20 (children under 5).

THE FACILITIES: Two sanitary blocks, a pool, playground, TV room and on-site restaurant, serving salads, omelettes and meat dishes.

FOOD AND DRINK: In Le Bar-sur-Loup, Le Jarrerie (00 33 4 93 42 92 92; www.restaurant-la-jarrerie.com) has to be visited. Set in an old stone monastery, it serves great French dishes and has a fixed *menu* deal for €27. There are also markets on Saturday mornings in Le Bar-sur-Loup, and a larger one in Valbonne on Friday mornings.

FAMILY FUN: Marineland in Antibes (00 33 4 93 33 49 49; www.marineland.fr), one of the largest marine attractions in Europe, is not far and has dolphin and sea-lion shows as well as a shark tunnel-aquarium. Fantastic.

TREAT YOURSELF: To some pampering at the Bastide Saint Antoine in Grasse (00 33 4 93 70 94 94; www.jacques-chibois.com), a Relais & Chateaux hotel with pool, jacuzzi, spa, *boules* pitch and cooking classes.

GETTING THERE: From Nice follow signs to Cagnes/Cannes/Aix-en-Provence, and merge onto the A8. Take exit 48 toward Cagnes-sur-Mer/Vence, and merge into the D336. Follow signs to Le Bar-sur-Loup, then signs to Camping Gorges du Loup.

PUBLIC TRANSPORT: Buses run from Grasse and Cannes to Le Bar-sur-Loup regularly. Local buses run right by the site several times a day and stop on request.

OPEN: Late-Mar–late-Sept.

IF IT'S FULL: The *Cool Camping* site at La Camassade (see p242) has fewer facilities but makes up for it in a more relaxed atmosphere.

Camping Les Gorges du Loup, 95 chemin des Vergers, 06620 Le Bar-sur-Loup

t 00 33 4 93 42 43 06 | w www.lesgorgesduloup.com

11

la camassade

Socrates once claimed: 'to be is to do'. Several hundred years later the philosopher Jean-Paul Sartre rejoined: 'to do is to be'. Frank Sinatra, perhaps unwittingly, fused these ideas when he sang 'do be do be do'. What has that got to do with camping, you may ask? Well the great news is that doers, thinkers and singers alike will all appreciate La Camassade's effortless tranquillity.

Set amidst olive and oak trees, with nothing to distract you from your thoughts but the occasional squirrel or fox, the site makes even its most understated neighbours seem like Butlins. It's a perfect spot to talk with the animals, wrestle with existentialism or simply get fit and active by taking advantage of the surrounding nature.

Born explorers will love it here: the site is well-placed for everything from hiking (more than 40 paths lie in the immediate vicinity) and fishing (in the River Loup a few miles away) or even airier thrills such as hang-gliding and paragliding, which can be enjoyed at Les Courmettes and Gourdon.

This well-loved site has been in the Dubois family for 34 years. Nowadays, Gérard and his son Alain maintain the site and did some rebuilding and restructuring a couple of years ago to promote their rural-hideaway philosophy.

This sanctuary of solitude has just 40 pitches, which are between an adequate 90 sq. m and a coolly colossal 200 sq. m in size. There's also a smattering of mobile homes, hordes of lovely, leafy trees, a swimming pool for cooling off (it's warm here for much of the year) and a small grocery shop that sells fresh bread and croissants that are baked on site.

You will have, no doubt, noticed the striking village of Tourrettes-sur-Loup on your way to the site – this 11th-century medieval village is famous for violets, artist studios, chapels and the Florian confectionary factory – great for sweet tooths, but even better for the kids as they can take a tour to see how the sweets are made.

The whole region is pretty arty – Saint-Paul de Vence and Vence itself have been associated with brush-wielding heavyweights, such as Matisse, Renoir, Modigliani, and writers such as Gide, Cocteau and Prévert. The typical Provençal towns and villages around are immediately charming, brimming with restaurants and boutiques – and, like a certain brand of beer, reassuringly expensive.

Cheaper thrills abound, too. You can hike out and admire the cliffs and waterfalls of the staggering Gorges du Loup, which cut north to south through the hills near Gourdon. And not far from there is the handsome old town of Grasse, once the world's perfume capital. There are numerous 'perfumeries' in Grasse, such as Fragonard and Galimard, each with tours and a museum.

Ten miles (15 km) beyond Grasse and you're in Cannes – film buffs might want to mark down May as a good time to visit the area so they can catch the lauded film festival. The French Riviera is, of course, on the doorstep. As, for that matter, is Italy, which is just an hour's drive away. Hard-core walkers can organise a two- to three-day trek directly from the site, which includes a sleepover on the Italian side of the Alps.

Come winter and spring, snowboarders and skiers may want to do some blue sky thinking and consider making this their base – instead of the usual Trois Vallées or Val d'Isère. As the weather is good most of the year round, you could rent a chalet or mobile home fairly cheaply – the closest ski slopes are just 45 minutes away.

Indeed, the surrounding topography makes La Camassade a great option for anyone seeking an action-packed holiday, whilst its natural ambience makes it equally alluring for those who want a serious chill out. Do Be Do Be Do? The choice is yours...

THE UPSIDE: Leafy, peaceful site with superb access to both culture and nature.

THE DOWNSIDE: No on-site entertainment or restaurant.

THE DAMAGE: A pitch is €6.80–10.30 per night; adults are €4.15–4.60 and children €2.05–2.25, depending on the season.

THE FACILITIES: There's a pool and a TV room but no restaurant. Both the showers and toilets are heated.

FOOD AND DRINK: Les Bacchanales in Tourrettes-sur-Loup (21 Grand Rue; 00 33 4 93 24 19 19) serves traditional dishes made from local market ingredients. And in Vence, Le Relais des Coches (00 33 4 93 24 31 24; www.lerelaisdescoches.com) combines great local food with a with a log-fire cosy ambience; plus, it doubles up as a jazz and blues bar at weekends.

FAMILY FUN: Funtrip in Pont du Loup are the people to call to organize everything from caving and canyoning to underwater dives and abseiling (00 33 6 19 66 03 65; www.funtrip.fr). Indulge your inner child if you don't have kids and visit the Confiserie Florian in Pont du Loup (00 33 4 93 59 32 91; www.confiserieflorian.com) – because there's no such thing as sweet enough.

TREAT YOURSELF: To a bird's eye view of the surroundings with some hang-gliding or paragliding at nearby Les Courmettes and Gourdon (see reception for details).

GETTING THERE: From Nice take the A8/E80 and follow the sign for Cagnes. At Cagnes-sur-Mer exit at junction 48 Cagnes-sur-Mer/Vence. After Vence take the D2210 (Route de Vence) to Tourrettes-sur-Loup. Then follow the signs for La Camassade.

PUBLIC TRANSPORT: From Nice you can get to Vence by bus, and from Vence to Tourette-sur-Loup there are four buses a day.

OPEN: All year.

IF IT'S FULL: The *Cool Camping* site of Les Gorges du Loup (see p240) is in the nearby town of Bar-sur-Loup.

Camping La Camassade, 523 Route de Pie Lombard, 06140 Tourrettes-sur-Loup

	t	00 33 4 93 59 31 54	w	www.camassade.com

Quechua

les romarins

Imagine waking up in the morning, unzipping your tent and watching honeyed sunrays skid lambently across the azure ripples of the Mediterranean. Imagine sipping your coffee whilst spying the private yachts of millionaires snaking in and out of Cap Ferrat harbour. Welcome to Les Romarins campsite, a sure winner of the *Cool Camping* award for Best Sea View in France – if such an award existed. *Cool Camping* Awards? Now, there's an idea.

High up in the hills between Nice and Monaco, Les Romarins is in the most remarkable of settings, where each of the 41 pitches boasts panoramic Mediterranean views. But it's the vibe as well as the view that gets into your soul – with no swimming pool, kids' activities or any loud entertainment, this really is a place to come and chill.

You'll need a car, though, not only to get to the site and nearby attractions, but also to whiz around the three *corniche* roads that cling to the curves of the coastal cliffs. The *Basse Corniche* snakes through the seafront Riviera towns, the *Grande Corniche* takes a faster, straighter line across the cliff tops, but it's the *Moyenne Corniche* that's said to be one of the most romantic drives in the world. Choose some suitable cruising music and put your foot down, this is the stuff of car ads and movie chases, with slaloms, hairpins – and more of those big, blue views around every bend.

The *Moyenne Corniche* will take you to the village of Èze, a pretty, medieval place perched high on a rock 475 metres above the sea. Its fortified castle was sadly destroyed in the 18th century (obviously not fortified enough) but the ruins now house the Jardin Exotique – a garden filled with exotic plants and cacti and with another stunning Riviera backdrop.

There are many other coastal towns to explore nearby. Villefranche-sur-Mer has one of the most beautiful bays along this stretch and has retained its ancient charms. You could easily spend a day sunbathing on the sand and pebble beach, becoming acquainted with the architecture of its 16th-century citadel or just sipping coffee by the harbour as the fishing boats bob and knock in the handsome dock.

Of course, you can't come here without visiting those Riviera jewels, Monaco and Nice, both just a short drive from the site. Where tiny Monaco is flash, swanky and swish, Nice is more traditional and relaxed with a characterful old town of narrow alleys to explore and plenty of places to sample local seafood specialities – without

EUROHIKE

the superstar price tag. Nice also has a long, pebbly beach with comfortable sunloungers for hire and waiters on hand to bring refreshments, but a bit of effort and a good map is all that's required to find the smaller, quieter beaches amongst the cliffs and coves between Monaco and Nice.

When you've had your fill of glitz and glamour, Les Romarins is a stunning location to return to every evening. The hill on which the site rests is dotted with rosemary and olive trees providing shade from the hot Mediterranean sun. The owners, who live on-site, ensure that the select clientele respect the tranquil nature of the place, and whilst the facilities are low-key, there is a snack bar with a panoramic terrace, a chill-out room and renovated washrooms. There's even an ironing board available to press that starched white shirt for a visit to the casino in Monaco – or perhaps for an awards ceremony?

THE UPSIDE: Chilled-out campsite views just don't get better than this.

THE DOWNSIDE: The small pitches and quiet vibe aren't really suitable for families.

THE DAMAGE: Pitches cost €16.30–19.10 per night for 2 people and a tent (depending on season). An extra adult costs between €5.45 and €6.75; children (under 5) are €3–3.50.

THE FACILITIES: The panoramic terrace and modern toilet block rock, and there's also a washing machine and public telephone.

FOOD AND DRINK: With only snacks and breakfast available on site, the closest place for a meal is Èze, which fortunately has plenty of cafés and restaurants. Château Eza is a romantic hotel with a wonderful Michelin-starred restaurant (rue de la Pise; 00 33 4 93 41 12 24; www.chateaueza.com); for a less-expensive option try Le Troubador, which serves great meat and lamb dishes in a medieval house and once entertained Robert Mitchum.

FAMILY FUN: Apart from the nearby beaches, Les Artistes du Soleil in Nice (16–18 boulevard de la République; 00 33 4 93 52 55 89) is an artistic and ceramic centre with kids' workshops on Wednesdays and school holidays. The Mini Center (4 rue Rancher; 00 33 6 18 21 06 20) in Vieux Nice organises activities for children.

TREAT YOURSELF: To the heady mixture of romance and roulette at one of Monaco's famous Monte Carlo Casinos (www.casino-montecarlo.com). If you don't have the money (or the jacket-and-tie to hand), perhaps a scuba dive might be a memorable souvenir of the Côte d'Azur (00 33 4 93 89 42 44; www.nicediving.com)?

GETTING THERE: From Nice take the Corniche André de Joly (D6007) and follow the *Moyenne Corniche*, turning off at avenue des Caroubiers (D33) to get to the site.

PUBLIC TRANSPORT: Buses run regularly from Nice and Monaco to Èze.

OPEN: mid-Apr–mid-Sept.

IF IT'S FULL: No other site comes close to the views, so change your dates and make a reservation.

Camping Les Romarins, Grande Corniche, 06360 Èze	t	00 33 4 93 01 81 64	w	www.campingromarins.com

useful info

Got the tent, got the sleeping bag, stove and corkscrew packed...Don't forget our top tips to keep your cool on those balmy French nights.

THE RIGHT SITE

Know the difference between an *aire naturelle* (a campsite with a small number of pitches on a farm or agricultural property) and a *camping naturiste* (nudist campsite) if you don't want to bare it all. For kids and campers keen to dip into local life, nothing beats the intimacy of a *camping à la ferme*. Limited to six *emplacements* (pitches) for 20 campers, it's an open invitation to hang out with the farmer, taste his produce, admire his animals and congratulate *Cool Camping* on yet another fabulous find. The quintessential, government-starred campsite in France – which we've avoided – is a vast, pool-clad amusement park rammed with caravans, mobile homes and people.

THE RIGHT TIME

If you can, skip French school holidays when much of France pitches up too. Spring holidays in April and October/November are reasonably quiet, but campsites burst in July and August. If you have to pick between the two, go for July – as early as possible – and bag your slot on site well in advance. Campsites generally open March to September or October. Speaking of the right time, France is always one hour ahead of the UK.

RAIN, HAIL OR SHINE

Watch the weather, particularly in mountainous areas and in the south where summer storms can be sudden, frequent and fierce. To check the weather forecast, call 3250; surf www.meteo.fr/meteonet_en; or type your campsite's postcode into the main body of a text message and send it to 73250.

ON THE ROAD

Motorists drive on the right, and vehicles coming from the right have priority.
Get that and driving in France can be a pleasure. Roads are quieter than in the UK, roundabouts abound to slow down speed fiends, and there are soul-stirring country lanes and *cols* (mountain passes) loaded with hairpin bends to hug.

Speed limits are 50 km/h (30 mph) in built-up areas, 90 km/h (55 mph) on the open road, 110 km/h (70 mph) on dual carriageways and 130 km/h (80 mph) on *autoroutes* (motorways) – which cost.
To calculate *péages* (tolls) pump *votre itinéraire* (your itinerary) into www.autoroutes.fr.
Children under 10 are not allowed to sit in the front seat and must be in an appropriate car seat in the back. Chatting

on your mobile whilst driving lands an immediate fine and the drink-drive limit is equivalent to two glasses of wine. Avoid buying the pricey petrol (*essence*) on the *autoroute*; rather try a supermarket on a town's outskirts. Leaving the *autoroute* for a spot of lunch likewise leaves a sweeter taste in your mouth.

Motoring on traffic-jammed 'black' days in July and August is grim. Check traffic conditions in advance with Bison Futé (00 33 892 687 888, France 08 26 02 20 22, www.bison-fute.equipement.gouv.fr) and avoid peak times, particularly Saturday. On the road, tune into Radio 107.7 FM for the latest traffic news.

MAKING THAT CALL

If you're calling from the UK or from your mobile in France, dial the telephone number *Cool Camping* lists, including the international access code '00' and France country code '33'. Calling from a payphone in France, drop the '00 33' and add a '0' before the remaining nine-digit number; campsites and *tabacs* (newsagents) sell *télécartes* (phonecards). French telephone numbers have 10 digits and no area code.

POSTCARD HOME

It costs 60 cents to send a postcard to Britain. Stamps (*timbres*) are sold at *tabacs*, campsite shops and post offices, flagged with a canary-yellow 'La Poste' sign and open weekdays plus Saturday 'til noon. Count two to four days for Mum to get your card.

CULINARY NUGGETS

Good food and wine is a huge part of what camping in France is all about. Every village has a market heaped with fresh fruit, veg, herbs, fish and meat gagging to be chopped up and cooked on a campfire. Check also what the local farmer sells. Few shops open Sunday and most break for a long lunch on other days.

Bread accompanies every meal, though a *baguette* bought at sunrise is rock-hard by sunset. Buy just enough for breakfast and shop later for more; every *boulangerie* bakes several times a day and sells *une demi-baguette* (a half baguette) should a whole one be too long.

Some campsites serve dinner, a typically French fixed *menu* comprising an *entrée* (starter), *plat* (main course), *dessert* (pudding) and *fromage* (cheese) – in that order – for €6–20. Make sure you say '*Bon appetit*!' before digging in.

DOWN THE HATCH

Tap water and water in fountains is drinkable unless it's marked '*non potable*'. When savouring local café culture or dining out, don't feel obliged to order a bottle of Evian (still) or Perrier (sparkling); ordering *une carafe d'eau* (jug of tap water) is perfectly acceptable.

Alsatians aside, the French seldom drink beer or tea (bring your own tea bags – leave a French tea bag soaking several days and you still won't get the strength of an English cuppa!). The day is kick-started with *un café* (a short sharp espresso) or tamer *café au lait* (milky coffee), and wine accompanies pretty much everything else. Shopping for it – look for *dégustation* (tasting) signs – at *châteaux* (castles) and *domaines* (estates) in Bordeaux, Burgundy, Provence and other wine-making areas is one of those great French joys. *Santé!*

DOWN THE PAN

Women's is *Dames*, men's is *Hommes* and that's the straighforward bit. French toilets are not always what they seem. Stroll into a WC and gals', you might well find yourself parading past a man at a urinal en route to the toilet safely ensconced behind a closed door. Once in, devices range from bog-standard, British-style toilets to – shock, horror, how antiquated is that? – a pair of elephant feet on which you squat. Hold tight to anything in your pockets and stand well clear before flushing.

LEAVE NO TRACE

Dump your rubbish in the right place, preferably in recycling bins (glass in green; newspapers/magazines in blue; plastic, cardboard and beer cans in yellow). Only ever light fires in designated areas, respect the countryside and don't hassle or feed the wildlife.

WHAT TO DO IN AN EMERGENCY

(besides yelling '*AU SECOURS* (HELP)!'

Fire – call 18 from a landline or 112 from a mobile

Police (Gendarmerie) – call 17

Ambulance (SAMU) – call 15

Mountain rescue – call 112; better still note the number of the local mountain-rescue squad before setting out

Lost/stolen passport – report at the local police station and contact the British Embassy (01 44 51 31 00, www.britishembassy.gov.uk) in Paris to find the nearest British consulate to get a replacement

Lost/stolen credit card – call 08 92 70 57 05 or MasterCard 08 00 90 13 87, Visa 08 00 90 11 79

useful phrases

Campsite – un camping
Pitch – une emplacement
Large/small tent – une grande/petite tente
Camper van – un mobil-home/un camping-car
Caravan – une caravane
Facility block – le bloc sanitaire
Toilets/urinals – les WCs/urinoirs
Showers – les douches
Washing-up/laundry sink – un bac lave vaiselle/lave linge
Drinking water – eau potable
Recycling bins – les bacs de recyclage
Sleeping bag – un sac de couchage
Air mattress – un matelas d'air
Campfire – un feu de camp
Pink/white marshmallows – les guimauves roses/blanches
Camping Gaz canister – une bouteille de Camping Gaz
Corkscrew – un tire bouchon
Tin opener – une ouvre-boîte
Mallet – un maillet

Where is the nearest campsite?
Où est le camping le plus proche?

How much does it cost to pitch a tent here?
Combien coûte une nuit en camping avec tente?

It costs a fixed €15 a day for two adults, tent and car.
Nous avons un forfait journalier à €15 pour deux adultes avec tente et voiture.

Where are the recycling bins?
Où sont les bacs de recyclage?

Do you have a spare tent peg/tin opener/lighter or matches?
Avez-vous un piquet de tente/ouvre-boîte/un briquet de poche ou des allumettes?

Could someone please clean the toilets?
Pourriez vous faire nettoyer les toilettes s'il vous plaît?

There's no hot water.
Il n'y a pas d'eau chaude.

Help! Someone has stolen my towel/ wallet/clothes!
Au secours! Quelqu'un a volé ma serviette/ mon porte-monnaie/mes vêtements!

Where should I park?
Où est-ce que je peux me garer?

Is it OK to build a campfire here?
Est-ce qu'on peut faire un feu de camp ici?

What a beautiful view!
Quelle vue magnifique!

Where's a good place to eat around here?
Où est-ce qu'il y a un bon endroit pour manger ici?

Do you speak English?
Est-ce que vous parlez anglais?

Sorry, I don't speak French.
Désolé, je ne parle pas français.

No, it's a complete misconception that all English people are football hooligans and eat nothing but roast beef.
Non, ce n'est pas vrai que tous les anglais sont des hooligans et mangent du rosbif.

happy campers?

We hope you've enjoyed reading *Cool Camping France* and that it's inspired you to get out there.

The campsites featured in this book are a personal selection chosen by the *Cool Camping* team. None of the campsites has paid a fee for inclusion, nor was one requested, so you can be sure of an objective choice of sites and honest descriptions.

We have visited hundreds of campsites across France to find these, and we hope you like them as much as we do. However, it hasn't been possible to visit every single French campsite. So if you know of a special place that you think should be included, we'd like to hear about it.

Send us an email telling us the name and location of the campsite, some contact details and why it's special. We'll credit all useful contributions in the next edition and the best emails will receive a complimentary copy. Thanks and see you out there!

france@coolcamping.co.uk

Cool Camping France
Series Concept & Series Editor:
Jonathan Knight
Researched, written and photographed by:
Keith Didcock, Sam Pow and Paul Sullivan
Co-ordinating author: Nicola Williams
Additional photography: Rob Ditcher
Editor: Nikki Sims
Proofreader: Jessica Cowie
Design and artwork: Andrew Davis
Production: Catherine Greenwood,
Andrew Davis
PR: The Farley Partnership
Coordinator-in-Chief: Catherine Greenwood

Published by:
Punk Publishing, 3 The Yard, Pegasus Place,
London, SE11 5SD

Distributed by:
Portfolio Books, Suite 3/4, Great West House,
Great West Road, Brentford, Middlesex, TW8 9DF

Punk Publishing takes its environmental responsibilities seriously. This book has been printed on paper made from renewable sources and we continue to work with our printers to reduce our overall environmental impact. Wherever possible, we recycle, eat organic food and always turn the tap off when brushing our teeth.